BLACKS IN WHITE COLLEGES

Oklahoma's Landmark Cases

By GEORGE LYNN CROSS

University of Oklahoma Press : Norman

Also by George Lynn Cross:

The World of Ideas: Essays on the Past and Future (Introduction)

Library of Congress Cataloging in Publication Data

Cross, George Lynn.
    Blacks in white colleges: Oklahoma's landmark cases.

    Includes index.
        1. Oklahoma. University.   2.   College integration—
Law and legislation—Oklahoma.   I.   Title.
KF01592.2.C76   344'.76637'0798   75–1432
ISBN 0–8061–1266–2
ISBN 0–8061–1267–0 pbk.

Publication of this book has been aided by a grant from the Wallace C. Thompson Fund of the University of Oklahoma Foundation.

"*Neither race, ancestry nor color of skin should be pertinent. . . .*"—
NAACP ATTORNEYS, SPRING, 1950.

"*No separate treatment of Negro and white students . . . is equal. . . .*"
—JUSTICE ROBERT H. JACKSON, SPRING, 1950.

"*. . . so, I nominated myself chief guinea pig.*"—ADA LOIS SIPUEL FISHER.

"*A university is . . . for development of minds—not preservation of color lines.*"—HOWARD FRIEDMAN, JANUARY, 1948.

"*Equality under a segregated system . . . a legal fiction; a judicial myth.*"—THURGOOD MARSHALL, MARCH, 1947.

"*Exclusion of any one group on the basis of race automatically imputes a badge of inferiority to the excluded group—an inferiority which has no basis in fact.*"—New York Herald-Tribune, JANUARY 27, 1948.

"*. . . nor shall any state deprive any person of life, liberty, or property without due process of law, nor deny to any person . . . the equal protection of the laws.*"—FOURTEENTH AMENDMENT, UNITED STATES CONSTITUTION.

"*Second-class citizenship cannot exist.*"—HOWARD FRIEDMAN, JANUARY, 1948.

"*If universities . . . cannot practice the principles of democracy and illustrate them by example, where . . . will they be illustrated and practiced?*"—LAWRENCE H. SNYDER, MARCH, 1948.

"*Separate educational facilities are inherently unequal.*"—CHIEF JUSTICE EARL WARREN, 1954.

"*Segregation itself amounts to an unlawful discrimination.*"—THURGOOD MARSHALL.

"*. . . the only way to ensure . . . equal education . . . was to make the same education available to all.*"—GEORGE LYNN CROSS.

PREFACE

During the first half of the twentieth century strictly enforced segregation laws in the southern states prevented individuals of African descent from attending educational institutions with white students at any level, and most of the states had laws that prohibited or regulated the mixing of races in public conveyances and facilities. These laws remained in effect despite the Thirteenth, Fourteenth, and Fifteenth amendments to the Constitution, passed by Congress and ratified during the nineteenth century, and they survived the two civil-rights acts that Congress designed in the latter half of the century to ensure the enforcement of the three amendments.

In 1946 the National Association for the Advancement of Colored People (NAACP) selected the University of Oklahoma for test cases designed to establish that segregation laws were unconstitutional at the graduate level. Action was initiated on January 14, 1946, when Ada Lois Sipuel, a twenty-two-year-old Negro from Chickasha, Oklahoma, applied for and was denied admission to the university. Subsequently a test suit was filed on her behalf in the District Court of Cleveland

County, and thus began a four-year court struggle, later to involve other plaintiffs, including George W. McLaurin, a faculty member of Langston University at Langston, Oklahoma.

The issue—whether state laws could force segregation in higher education—was settled not only for the University of Oklahoma but for all colleges and universities of the country when the Supreme Court of the United States ruled in 1950 that such laws deprived citizens of their constitutional rights and could no longer be enforced.

The results of the Supreme Court's monumental decision were so important and far-reaching that it seemed worthwhile to describe in some detail the events at the University of Oklahoma that led, directly or indirectly, to that decision.

There had been, of course, prior attempts to challenge segregation in higher education. The closest parallel to the Oklahoma situation occurred in the neighboring state of Missouri, where Lincoln University was the public institution of higher learning established for Negroes under the state's segregation laws. The same laws provided that Negro students who sought programs of study not offered at Lincoln might have their tuition fees for such programs paid at institutions beyond the state's borders.

Robert Gaines graduated from Lincoln University in 1935 and, desiring a legal education, applied for admission to the School of Law at the University of Missouri. His application was denied by the registrar, who referred him to Lincoln University for assistance. At Lincoln, Gaines was advised that the governing board of the institution had the option of establishing a school of law for Negroes or paying his tuition in a northern school.

Gaines took his case through the state courts but found no relief. In 1938 his attorneys appealed the case to the Supreme Court of the United States. The Court ruled that the Missouri laws giving Lincoln University the option of providing educational programs for Negroes or paying out-of-state tuition for such programs in other states did not meet the constitutional requirement of equal protection and were discriminatory. The Court emphasized that the pivotal question in the case was not what other states provided by way of educational opportunities for Missouri citizens but rather what opportunities the state of Missouri provided for white students. The decision, in effect, required Missouri to provide a school of law for Negroes within the state, equal in quality to the school for white students.

Gaines and his attorneys did not pursue the case further, but in 1939, Lucille Bluford, a graduate of Lincoln University, applied for admission to the Graduate School of Journalism at the University of Missouri. The registrar, S. W. Canada, denied her admission, and promptly found himself the defendant in a suit for damages filed in the Federal District Court for the Western District of Missouri. In a decision given in April, 1940, the court referred to the Gaines case and the fact that, subsequently, the Missouri legislature had given Lincoln University the mandatory responsibility of providing educational facilities for Negroes comparable to those available at the University of Missouri. The court declared, however, that the failure of Lincoln "to keep and maintain in idleness and non-use facilities at Lincoln University which no one had requested or indicated a desire to use" could not be construed as a disregard of the rights of Negro citizens in Missouri. The court further stated that Missouri was within its rights if it wished to maintain "separate but equal" educational facilities and that the plaintiff did not have cause for complaint until she had "applied to the proper authorities for those rights" and had been unlawfully refused.

The effects of the decisions in the Gaines and Bluford cases were as follows: (1) the doctrine of "separate but equal" educational facilities for white and Negro students was upheld; (2) a state could not evade its responsibility for providing equal educational facilities for Negroes by paying the tuition of a Negro student who attended an institution outside of the state; and (3) a Negro student's rights to equal educational opportunities could not be considered denied until a request for educational opportunity had been made to the state and the request denied. These points were to become the basis for the defense of segregation at the University of Oklahoma. The defense failed when the United States Supreme Court concluded in 1950 that "separate but equal" educational opportunity was a concept impossible to achieve in practice and that the only way to ensure that equal educational opportunity would be available to all citizens was to make the same education available to everyone.

It is a pleasure to acknowledge those who gave help during the preparation of the following account. Ms. Barbara James, Secretary to the Board of Regents of the University of Oklahoma, graciously aided in finding the minutes of the meetings of the regents which had to do with action taken during the long legal struggle. Maurice H. Merrill, Research Professor Emeritus of Law, read the manuscript and gave many helpful, critical suggestions. Ms. Mary E. Stith, Editor of the University of Oklahoma Press, contributed suggestions concerning the organization of the manuscript. Charles Bennett, Managing Editor of the *Daily Oklahoman* and the *Oklahoma City Times*, provided many of the illustrations. Grateful acknowledgment for permission to reproduce them is made to Mr. Bennett and to the Oklahoma Publishing Company. I am indebted also to my wife, Cleo S. Cross, who provided many very useful suggestions and much-needed encouragement. Finally, I am grateful to my secretary, Ms. Robbye Meaders, who worked patiently at the job of typing and retyping, and who made numerous trips to the University Library in search of source materials.

Norman, Oklahoma

GEORGE LYNN CROSS
President Emeritus
University of Oklahoma

CONTENTS

ILLUSTRATIONS

BLACKS IN WHITE COLLEGES

I.

BACKGROUND

Decisions made during the spring and summer of 1934 caused me to become involved with the events described in the following pages. The first of these decisions came at the end of the second semester at the University of South Dakota, where I had spent four years as professor and head of the Department of Botany. During that four-year period, the middle-western states had been plagued by a prolonged drought accompanied by dust storms of a magnitude not previously experienced in the country. On many days the sky was so darkened by dust that the street lights, which could be seen only dimly at a distance of from thirty to forty feet, were kept turned on in the little city of Vermillion, where the university was situated.

The economy of South Dakota was almost entirely dependent upon agriculture. After four successive years of crop failure the state found itself with very serious financial problems. Appropriations for higher education were severely slashed. My salary had been reduced 35 per cent during my four years at the university, and the future seemed bleak. I gave a great deal of thought to the possibility of finding employment in an area with a more broadly based economy.

At the close of the school term my wife and I had approximately one hundred dollars in cash and still owed fifty dollars on a vacuum cleaner we had purchased. We discussed the possibility of a vacation trip in our automobile, which would take us out of the dust, at least for a time, and we weighed this carefully against the advisability of completing the payment for the vacuum cleaner. We decided to travel and a few days later were in the Black Hills of South Dakota, enjoying the fresh, clean air of those beautiful mountains.

After a few days of this kind of living we were reluctant to return to the dust of eastern Dakota, and we decided to push farther west for as long as our money held out. There appeared to be two interesting possibilities for additional travel: we could visit the Rocky Mountain biological station at Gothic, Colorado, or we could go to the summer camp for geology and biology maintained by the University of Wyoming, in the Snowy Range near Centennial, Wyoming. This called for a second decision —a fateful one—which we decided should be based on the flip of a coin. The coin's choice was the University of Wyoming summer camp, and we took off immediately. At the camp we met Professor Paul B. Sears, Chairman of the Department of Botany and Bacteriology at the University of Oklahoma. Professor Sears was looking for a structural botanist to succeed Professor Adriance Foster, who had left Oklahoma for a position at the University of California at Berkeley. Professor Sears offered me the position. Although the salary differential was approximately a hundred dollars and my title would be that of assistant professor, Mrs. Cross and I had little difficulty reaching a decision to accept the offer.

On the whole, the decision turned out to be a good one. During the late 1930's, Professor Sears left the University of Oklahoma to accept a position at Oberlin College, and I succeeded him as head of the Department of Botany and Microbiology. Shortly after the United States became involved in World War II, Professor Homer Dodge, Dean of the Graduate College, was called to Washington, D.C., to aid in the war effort, and I became Acting Dean of the Graduate College. When Joseph A. Brandt, President of the University, resigned in 1943 to accept the directorship of the University of Chicago Press, I was named Acting President. In 1944, I was named President, a post I held for nearly twenty-five years, during a period of many changes at the university—the most important of which certainly involved the events described in the following pages.

One summer afternoon in 1934, shortly after moving to Norman, I discussed with a local merchant several aspects of life in the community where my family and I expected to live for the next several years. During the course of our conversation the man introduced the subject of racial relations, with the comment that I would never need to worry about the "nigger problem." He made the remark with obvious pride, explaining that there were no Negroes living in Norman or even in the vicinity of Norman. There was an unwritten law, he said, that a Negro could not remain within the city limits after

sundown. This restriction had been in effect since the
settling of Norman during the land rush of 1889. I asked
how such an unwritten "law" could be enforced, and he
told me that there had never been need for enforcement.
The Negroes, he said, understood the situation perfectly
and knew better than to remain in the city after sundown. He then went on to explain that, while Negroes
were permitted to work in the city during the day, they
were never permitted to live there because their resi-
dential areas would certainly become slums that would
destroy the value of adjacent property owned by whites.
He described a few instances of how this had happened
in other municipalities where the citizenry had lacked
the foresight shown by the Normanites.

I was a little startled by what the man said, especially
by his hint about what might happen to a Negro caught
in Norman after sundown, but I considered his remarks
of only local significance. It did not occur to me that they
spotlighted attitudes that would cause almost over-
whelming problems in human relations during the decades to follow. As a matter of fact, it was not until I
became involved in preparing this book that I fully came
to understand the extent to which citizens of Norman
had gone, even in early territorial days, to convince
Negroes that Norman was not for them.[1]

Early in June, 1898, J. J. Wallace, a tinner and roofer
with a store and place of business in Oklahoma City,
came to Norman to perform some work in line with his
trade. He brought with him as an assistant a black named

[1] I am indebted to Maurice Merrill, Research Professor Emeritus of
Law in the University of Oklahoma, for the details of the Wallace case.

George Rogan. While engaged in their work, Wallace and his assistant allegedly were attacked by a group of approximately twenty-five persons who beat Wallace about the head, eyes, and body, knocked him senseless, fractured his skull, and caused him to lose the sight of his left eye. As a result of these injuries, he alleged, it was necessary for him to be under the care of a physician and nurse for sixty days, and he had been permanently incapacitated from successfully following his trade.

Wallace subsequently filed a twenty-five-thousand-dollar suit for damages in the District Court of Cleveland County against the town of Norman. Wallace contended in the petition that the attack on him was the result of a conspiracy on the part of the citizens of Norman to prevent, by threats of physical violence, the "laboring, living or lodging within the corporate limits of the defendant town of law-abiding colored citizens of the United States." He cited incidents that had occurred during the preceding three years when black citizens of the United States—Frank Rogan, Robert Green, David Branham, Robert Ely, and others whose names were unknown to him—had been assaulted, beaten, and driven from Norman when they attempted to work there. He alleged that the "defendant town, and all of its officers and agents" had knowledge of the conspiracy to keep Negroes from living or working in the area, basing his allegation on the fact that the town marshal, J. S. Davidson, had been present and had given audible encouragement when he, Wallace, had been beaten.

In November, 1898, the town of Norman filed a demurrer to Wallace's petition on the grounds that the petition did not state a cause of action. In September of the following year the district court sustained the demurrer.

Wallace then took his case to the Supreme Court of the Territory of Oklahoma, where the case was reviewed in January, 1900. The territorial Supreme Court, in an opinion handed down by Justice J. Irwin, sustained the action of the lower court on the grounds that the petition had not shown that the town of Norman had been remiss in not passing laws against the kind of attack upon which his petition was based. The town could not be held responsible for an attack by a group of individuals unless it could be shown that the town had been negligent in not passing such laws.[2] Apparently realizing the hopelessness of the situation, Wallace elected to drop the matter rather than take additional court action with a revised petition.

There were many undocumented rumors of Negroes having been run out of Norman during the first quarter of the twentieth century, but an authentic case, well remembered by several citizens of the community, occurred in the early 1920s, when V. V. Harris, a wealthy oilman of Oklahoma City, decided that he would like to attend the University of Oklahoma. Harris constructed a home at 518 South Lahoma and moved into it with his wife, two small children, and a Negro woman who had been a long-time member of the family. The Negro woman was housed in an apartment above the garage behind the house. Her duties were to take care of the house and look after the children; although she never

2 *Wallace* v. *Town of Norman*, 9 Okla. 339, 60 P. 138 (1900).

left the premises, her presence there was considered objectionable by some Norman residents. The Harris home was bombarded with rocks wrapped in paper on which messages were written. The messages thrown on the front and rear porches of the house read, in effect, "Get rid of the nigger or else!"[3]

The Harris family endured the harassment for a year or so but finally sold their home to a sorority and moved back to Oklahoma City. The sorority occupied the house for several years, during which period one of their members was Dorothy Wentz, a niece of Lew Wentz, a wealthy oilman who lived in Ponca City. Dorothy's automobile was driven by a Negro chauffeur. Possibly taking her cue from what had happened previously at the house, she kept her car and chauffeur in Oklahoma City, about twenty miles away.

William Bennett Bizzell became President of the University of Oklahoma in 1925, after serving for ten years as President of the Texas Agricultural and Mechanical College. Once, during his earlier years at the university, he was visited by friends from Texas, who arrived in Norman in an automobile driven by a Negro chauffeur. Since the friends would spend the night in the guest room at the president's home on Boyd Street, President Bizzell planned to have the Negro occupy the apartment above the garage in the rear of the home. News of the plan got around Norman by the middle of the afternoon, and by late afternoon the president had received so many threatening phone calls concerning the arrange-

[3] Related by Professor Maurice Merrill and corroborated by Mrs. Stephen Scatori, a neighbor of the Harris family.

ment that he sent the Negro chauffeur to Oklahoma City
to be housed for the night.

There is no recorded instance of a Negro having spent
the night within the city limits of Norman until the naval
installations were established in the town after the beginning of World War II. The local citizens apparently
realized that if they were to reap the financial benefits of
the presence of the two large bases it would be necessary
to accept the naval personnel regardless of race. In the
beginning an effort was made to keep Negroes out of
Norman housing, but this effort gradually failed as naval
officers came to the community with their families and
insisted on having Negro helpers on their premises.

My early incomprehension of the Oklahoma situation
perhaps stemmed from the fact that I had had almost
no contact with any member of the black race until I
entered South Dakota State College in the fall of 1923.
There I found myself a member of a football squad
which included one Negro—a fine halfback named Ross
Owens, whom our very aggressive coach, Jack West, had
recruited from Fort Scott, Kansas. Charlie, as Ross was
known by everyone on the campus, was a splendid ath-
lete and a very intelligent young man with a fine sense of
humor. I don't remember anyone ever suggesting that it
was undesirable to have a Negro on the squad. Participa-
tion of Negroes in athletics was not uncommon in northern universities at that time, although they had not as
yet found acceptance in professional sports. When our
team traveled, Charlie always shared a room with some
member of the squad, and there appeared to be little

awareness that he was of different racial origin. My first experience with segregation came on an occasion when Charlie was refused a hotel room in Sioux City, Iowa. The reaction of his teammates was immediate and unanimous—they would not stay in the hotel. The coach spent an hour or so on the phone before finding accommodations for us elsewhere. This was the only problem of its kind that we encountered over a three-year period, although we read frequently of racial problems in the larger cities of the country, especially the northern cities. On the whole, from our isolated position, it appeared that such problems, while temporarily frustrating and embarrassing, would surely find ultimate solutions.

But in Oklahoma, as in other southern states, the situation was complicated by the fact that there were laws that prohibited mixing of the races. Negroes could not attend white schools at any educational level. They had their own grade schools, secondary schools, and a single, unaccredited institution of higher learning, Langston University, which had been established in 1897 as the Agricultural and Normal University for Negroes.

Of course, when one considers the historical background of Oklahoma, it is understandable—almost inevitable—that this should have been the case. With the exception of the Panhandle, Oklahoma was part of a tract of land acquired by the United States from France in 1803. Negro slavery had existed in the territory, especially in the southern portion, before its purchase by the United States. A clause in the purchase agreement, which guaranteed the protection of the liberties, property, and religion of the inhabitants, classified slaves as property and thus provided a legal basis for the continuance of slavery there after the purchase.[4]

When Maine and Missouri were admitted to the Union through congressional enactment of the Missouri Compromise, the act provided that slavery was to be barred north of latitude 36°30′ but that land south of this line should be slave territory. Slavery, therefore, received direct legal sanction in what is now Oklahoma.

In the meantime since 1817 the federal government had been developing plans for the removal of the Five Civilized Tribes from their former homes in the southeastern states to the Indian Territory—ultimately to become Oklahoma. This removal was completed for the most part by 1842. The Five Civilized Tribes, following the practices of their white neighbors in the southern states, had adopted the custom of Negro slavery, and when they were removed to their new homes, they took their slaves with them. Under the terms of the various treaties incident to the acquisition of the new territory and the removal of the Indians to it, the Indians were free to manage their slaves as they saw fit until the end of the Civil War. While there was considerable variation in the degree of segregation developed by the different tribes, few if any Negroes attained the rights of citizens in the tribes; correspondingly, few if any received the right to attend the schools that were developed in the newly occupied areas.

Political philosophy, social tradition, and various eco-

---

[4] Ollie Everett Hatcher, "The Development of Legal Controls in Racial Segregation in the Public Schools of Oklahoma, 1865–1952" (Ph.Ed. diss., University of Oklahoma, 1954), 23.

nomic factors tended to cause the tribes to cast their lots with the Confederacy during the Civil War. This was particularly the case with the Choctaws and Chickasaws. The Cherokees, Creeks, and Seminoles were somewhat divided on the issue, however, and the Cherokees and Creeks organized "governments in exile." This may have also been true of the Seminoles. John Ross, an influential member of the Cherokee tribe, tried for a time to maintain neutrality for his people, but eventually he was pressured to recognize the South. Ultimately all the tribes entered into treaties with the southern states, and they took part in the combat against the North. At the end of the war it was inevitable that they should share the consequences of defeat with their southern allies.

In 1866, almost immediately after the cessation of hostilities, the federal government took up the matter of dealing with its insubordinate subjects. It took the position that the real governments of the five tribes were those that adhered to the Confederacy and that their disloyalty provided justification for abrogating the older treaties that guaranteed certain rights to the tribes. Under the new treaties the Five Civilized Tribes were forced to return to the federal domain for what appears to have been inadequate consideration—roughly the western one-half of their territory. The land reclaimed by the federal government was used to further its policy of forcing the Plains tribes onto reservations and to achieve a concentration of other tribes already on reservations that had become something of a "nuisance" in the eyes of the white inhabitants of the older states.

Thus what was to become Oklahoma consisted of

approximately equal halves, the eastern half known as Indian Territory, and the western as Oklahoma Territory. Many Indian tribes, driven from their original homes by the western march of the whites, were settled in the Oklahoma Territory. However, it should be pointed out that the area was not officially designated Oklahoma Territory until 1890, when Congress passed the Organic Act for the Territory of Oklahoma. This act established the new territory as consisting of the lands taken from the Five Civilized Tribes by the treaties of 1866, plus the addition of what was known as No Man's Land, the present Panhandle of Oklahoma. Thus, from 1890, two territorial entities existed side by side in what is now Oklahoma. They were commonly referred to as the Twin Territories.

There were interesting differences in the governmental structures of the two territories. While both were subject to the provisions of the United States Constitution and the Indian affairs of both were supervised and controlled by a federal authority, the Territory of Oklahoma, under the terms of the Organic Act, had a single central government with provision for local self-government characteristic of other territories of the United States. This was in marked contrast to the situation in the Indian Territory, where five semisovereign nations existed, each with its own powers, although modified by treaties with the federal government.

While in the beginning the area which comprised the two territories had been occupied predominantly by Indians, there had been considerable infiltration of white intruders through the years. White traders had found their way into the Indian Territory early in the nine-teenth century. Later, when railroads were constructed in both territories, gangs of laborers and other personnel associated with the railroads were brought into the terri-tories, and many of them remained. Sightseers and ad-venturers also came in large numbers.

The white influx into Indian Territory was encour-aged to some extent by certain economically aggressive Indians who had developed large-scale farming and ranching operations in the territory. These Indians changed their system to one which, in effect, involved sharecropping. They leased their lands mostly to whites who had moved into the areas from the states south and east of the Indian Territory, where, for one reason or an-other, they had been unable to secure access to land. James Lafayette Roberts, the father-in-law of Maurice H. Merrill, came to Indian Territory under such an arrange-ment as a tenant farmer under an Indian landlord.[5] In 1885, Indian agent Robert Owen reported 25,000 whites in the area occupied by the Five Civilized Tribes, and five years later agent Leo E. Bennett reported 140,000 whites in a total population of approximately 210,000.[6]

Additional impetus to settlement of whites in Okla-homa Territory was given when areas were opened by "runs" in 1889, 1891, and 1895 and by lottery in 1901. Ultimately the white population came to outnumber the Indians by a ratio of four, or perhaps even five, to one. This racial imbalance, coupled with the fact that in

[5] Memorandum from Professor Merrill.
[6] Edwin C. McReynolds, *Oklahoma: A History of the Sooner State* (Norman, University of Oklahoma Press, 1954), 277.

15

the areas outside of incorporated towns there were no revenues to support schools for white children or provide public improvements, was the principal factor in the demand for statehood that developed during the late nineteenth and early twentieth centuries.

While revenues for the support of education were sparse at the time, provision ultimately had been made for some financing. The Organic Act set aside the fifteenth and thirty-sixth sections of land in each township of the territory for the support of elementary education, as was the custom when public lands were occupied. In the Cherokee outlet two additional sections, the thirteenth and thirty-third, were set aside, one for higher education and one for public buildings.[7]

Following the Civil War the United States government took positive steps, through constitutional amendment and congressional legislation, to guarantee the political and social rights of all citizens. The Thirteenth Amendment, which prohibited slavery and involuntary servitude within the limits of the United States—"except as a punishment for crime whereof the party shall have been fully convicted"—had been ratified by twenty-seven states by December, 1863. This amendment was followed in 1866 by the first Civil Rights Act, which conferred citizenship upon Negroes and granted the same civil rights to all persons born in the United States—except Indians. Such legislation was deemed necessary because of the Dred Scott decision in 1857, when the United States Supreme Court ruled that Scott (and therefore all Negro slaves or their descendants) was not

[7] *Ibid.*, 301.

The Board of Regents and the president of the University of Oklahoma, shown above, were defendants in the litigation in the segregation cases. Front row, left to right: Judge William R. Wallace, Oklahoma City; Ned Shepler, Lawton; Joe W. McBride, Anadarko; President George Lynn Cross. Back row, left to right: Dr. Oscar White, Oklahoma City; Don Emery, Bartlesville; Lloyd Noble, Ardmore; Erl Deacon, Cushing; Emil Kraettli, secretary of the board, Norman. Courtesy University of Oklahoma Archives, Norman.

LEFT TO RIGHT: President Cross, Vice-President Carl Mason Franklin, Vice-President Roscoe Cate, and John B. Cheadle, legal adviser to the president and regents. Courtesy University of Oklahoma Archives.

Mac Q. Williamson, state attorney general of Oklahoma, handled the cases for the defense. Courtesy *Oklahoman and Times*, Oklahoma City.

Fred Hansen, assistant state attorney general, appeared for the defense in all court sessions. Courtesy *Oklahoman and Times*.

20

Maurice H. Merrill, professor of law and dean of the School of Law, assisted in preparing the defense. Courtesy *Sooner Yearbook*, University of Oklahoma.

John B. Cheadle, professor of law and legal adviser to the president and regents, also helped with the defense. Courtesy University of Oklahoma Archives.

Roy J. Turner (seated, shown here with President Cross) became governor of Oklahoma in January, 1947. He was cooperative and helpful during the long court struggle. Courtesy Office of Media Information, University of Oklahoma.

Roscoe Dunjee, editor of the *Black Dispatch*, Oklahoma City, and state president and national director of the NAACP, was the first to challenge the "separate but equal" doctrine during the litigation involving the University of Oklahoma. From the beginning he insisted that "equal" opportunity was possible only when the same education was available to both blacks and whites. Courtesy *Oklahoman and Times*.

a citizen of the United States, and thus was not entitled to sue in the federal courts.

As a result of widespread doubt concerning the constitutionality of the first Civil Rights Act, the Fourteenth Amendment was passed by Congress in 1866 and was ratified by the states in 1868. This amendment guaranteed the rights of citizenship to Negroes by declaring that "all persons born or naturalized in the United States, and subject to the jurisdiction thereof, are citizens of the United States and of the State wherein they reside." It went on to provide that no state shall "deprive any person of life, liberty, or property without due process of law, nor deny to any person within its jurisdiction the equal protection of the laws."

The Thirteenth and Fourteenth amendments would appear to have ensured protection of the individual rights of citizens regardless of race, creed, color, or ethnic origin, but difficulties soon developed in some of the southern states concerning interpretation of the disfranchising clauses. In response to the problem Congress proposed the Fifteenth Amendment, which guaranteed suffrage to every citizen. The Fifteenth Amendment was ratified by the states in 1870.

To ensure the complete enforcement of the provisions of the three amendments, Congress passed the second Civil Rights Act in 1875. This act guaranteed equal rights to all citizens in public places—inns, public conveyances, theaters, and so on—without distinction based on color, and specifically prohibited the exclusion of Negroes from jury duty. But in 1883 the Supreme Court held that this act was invalid when social rather than political rights were involved. Basing its decision upon the structure of the Fourteenth Amendment, the Court held that the act prohibited the invasion of civil rights by the states but did not protect against the invasion of civil rights by individuals. The decision left the federal government virtually powerless to intercede in situations in which the rights of Negroes were violated by private individuals.

The first government of Oklahoma Territory was organized in 1890 under procedures prescribed by the Organic Act. President Benjamin Harrison appointed George W. Steele of Indiana as the territory's first governor. Steele reported for duty at Guthrie, which had been named by the Organic Act as the territorial capital, and arranged for a general election of territorial legislators to be held on August 5. The legislature went into session three weeks after the election.

During its first meeting the legislators spent much of their time in controversy over the location of the territorial capital and of territorial institutions of higher learning, but they dealt also with the development of a public-school system—elementary and some high schools —for the various towns and townships. In preparing the laws necessary for the implementation of a system of public education, a struggle developed over the question of segregation of Negroes in the schools. By way of compromise, when the laws were finally enacted, segregation was left to local option, to be determined by popular vote at the county level on the first Tuesday of April, 1891, and every three years thereafter. This policy of segregation by local option was to remain in effect until 1897.

Late in December, 1890, the legislature established

three institutions of higher learning in the territory: the University of Oklahoma at Norman, the Agricultural and Mechanical College at Stillwater, and the Normal School at Edmond. Surprisingly, the acts establishing these institutions made no provision for segregation. It was provided that the university would be "open to female as well as male students" under regulations to be prescribed by the Board of Regents. At the Agricultural and Mechanical College admission was open to "all citizens of the territory of Oklahoma between the ages of 12 and 30" upon application. Admission to the Normal School at Edmond was left to a board of education, which was given the authority to develop "such rules and regulations for the admission of pupils" as the board might "deem necessary and proper." Thus there was no legal reason why Negroes could not have attended the newly established institutions of higher learning in the territory, but the fact that none did attend suggests that extralegal controls may have been operative.

The period of "local option" for the admission of Negroes to elementary and secondary schools, with no legal barriers to their admission to institutions of higher learning in the territory, lasted only until 1897. It ended during the fourth regular session of the territorial legislature, when a law was passed that ended the local-option principle and prescribed segregated educational programs for the territory. The new statute provided that "it shall hereafter be unlawful for any white child to attend a colored school or any colored child to attend any white school." Thus the doctrine of "separate but equal" educational facilities for the black and white races became

operative in Oklahoma Territory and continued until the
twin territories were united in 1907 to become the state
of Oklahoma.

The Enabling Act (Hamilton Bill), passed by Congress in 1906, authorized the Territory of Oklahoma and
the Indian Territory to organize a state government, develop a constitution, and be admitted to the Union as a
state. The act provided that the constitution of the new
state should protect its citizens against "distinction in
civil or political rights on account of race or color" and
that a system of public education should be developed
"open to all of the children of the state." But in establishing this requirement, the act went on to state that "this
shall not be construed to prevent the establishment and
maintenance of separate schools for white and colored
children." From either a philosophical or a rational point
of view, it would be difficult to reconcile this latter provision with previous congressional legislation—constitutional amendments and acts having to do with the rights
of individuals—but the Enabling Act clearly gave the
new state of Oklahoma a choice in the matter of educational segregation.

The Enabling Act, signed by President Theodore
Roosevelt on June 16, 1906, provided that a constitutional convention should be formed, with 112 delegates
to be elected. The election of delegates was held on
November 6, 1906, and the delegates went to work
immediately, with William H. Murray as president. The
first article of the new constitution provided for the
development of a system of public schools to be opened
to all children of the state but did not preclude "the

establishment and maintenance of separate schools for white and colored children." Article XIII was somewhat more specific; it provided that "separate schools for white and colored with like accommodations shall be provided by the legislature and impartially maintained." Article XXIII included an attempt to clarify the distinction between "white and colored" children by specifying that

wherever in this Constitution and laws of this State the word or words "colored" or "colored race," "negro" or "negro race," are used the same shall be construed to mean or apply to all persons of African descent. The term "white race" shall include all other persons.

This oversimplification of racial distinction left unclear the question whether a white child born on the African continent would be considered "colored" for the purpose of enrollment in Oklahoma's educational system or whether a person with some measure of Negro blood but not of African descent would be considered white for the same purpose.

Perhaps owing to oversight, the constitution made no provision for racial segregation in the institutions of higher learning. However, this was accomplished by the first Oklahoma legislature in 1908, when legislation was enacted providing that "it shall be unlawful for any person, corporation or association of persons, to maintain or operate any college, school or institution of this state where persons of both the white and colored races are received as pupils for instruction." The legislation included a further clarification of the term "colored," which had been used somewhat ambiguously in the constitution, by declaring that the term meant "all persons of African descent, who possessed any quantum of Negro blood," but it retained the rather dubious provision that the term white "should include all other persons." While additional legislation concerning the segregation of Negroes was to be forthcoming in future years, the state constitution and the enactments of the first legislature remained the principal legal barriers to the mixing of races in the schools of Oklahoma during the remainder of the first half of the twentieth century.

Negroes understandably resented this discrimination, but the depth of their resentment did not become apparent to me until late in the summer of 1945, when it was announced in the newspapers that a meeting of the National Association for the Advancement of Colored People was scheduled to be held in McAlester, Oklahoma, early in September of that year. Among those who attended the meeting were such distinguished Negro leaders as Thurgood Marshall, of New York, attorney for the NAACP, and Roscoe Dunjee, editor of the *Black Dispatch*, a Negro newspaper published in Oklahoma City.

After the session ended on Saturday, September 3, Marshall announced that a decision had been reached to test Oklahoma's segregation laws in the courts. His announcement was widely publicized in the Sunday newspapers the following day. Marshall said that an attempt would be made to enroll Negro students in the University of Oklahoma and Oklahoma A&M College and that students who wanted courses at the graduate level or in professional programs not offered at Langston

University would be selected for the test cases. He inti-
mated that the plan for attacking the state laws would
be similar to the one that had been used with some suc-
cess by Negroes in the state of Missouri in the Lloyd
Gaines case. Gaines, after graduating from Lincoln University, applied for admission to the University of Missouri. When he was denied admission, he took his case
through the courts and eventually to the Supreme Court
of the United States. The high court, in an opinion
announced by Chief Justice Charles Evans Hughes on
December 12, 1938, ruled that Gaines either must be
admitted to the University of Missouri law school or a
separate law school must be set up for Negroes at Lincoln
University.[8]

Perhaps in an attempt to ward off similar efforts to
attack segregation in Oklahoma, the state legislature,
following the Gaines decision appropriated funds at each
legislative session for the use of Negro students who
found it necessary to leave the state to pursue courses of
study not offered at Langston University.

Roscoe Dunjee, in an interview the same Saturday
evening, September 3, said that the first effort of his
group would be to get Langston University accredited
for the courses it was offering at the time. He stated,
however, that he was opposed to separate schools for
Negroes and whites because they "operate on the theory
that one human being is better than another."

The news stories following the McAlester meeting
caused something of a furor in local higher-education
circles. The regents of the University of Oklahoma met

[8] *Missouri* ex rel. *Gaines* v. *Canada*, 305 U.S. 337 (1938).

on November 7, 1945, a week earlier than they would have met under normal circumstances, to discuss the problems faced by their institution.

It was brought out during the meeting of the board that the Oklahoma constitution provided for the maintenance of separate schools for Negroes[9] and that statutes passed by the state legislature in 1941[10] (in part a reenactment of the legislation by the first Oklahoma legislature) prohibited Negro students from attending the schools of Oklahoma, including the University of Oklahoma. The statutes also made it a misdemeanor for a school administrator to admit Negro students to a white school, to instruct classes composed of mixed races, or to attend classes composed of mixed races. The law provided in effect that the president of the University of Oklahoma would be guilty of a misdemeanor if he admitted a Negro to the university and that punishment for violation of the law would be a fine of not less than one hundred dollars and not more than five hundred dollars, each day of violation being a separate offense; that instructors who taught mixed classes would be subject to a fine of not less than ten dollars or more than fifty dollars, each day a separate offense; that a white student who attended mixed classes would be subject to a fine of not less than four dollars or more than twenty dollars, each day a separate offense.

After discussing the problem thoroughly, Regent William R. Wallace, of Oklahoma City, moved that "the Board of Regents instruct the President of the University

9 Sec. 3, Art. XIII.
10 70 Okla. Stat. 1941, Sec. 452–64.

to refuse to admit anyone of Negro blood as a student in the University."[11] Wallace's motion was passed unanimously. It was then a matter of waiting for the appearance of the first Negro applicant for admission.

The announcement by the officials of the National Association for the Advancement of Colored People that Oklahoma's segregation laws would be tested in the courts and that the University of Oklahoma was one of the institutions selected for the test brought to my office a great deal of mail and many phone calls. There was an abundance of advice about how the problem should be handled when the first Negro applicant appeared for admission. All the communications seemed based on the assumption that the university had freedom of choice in the matter, despite the segregation laws, and they were about equally divided between those who opposed admission of Negroes and those who favored it. Many of the letters from those who opposed desegregation were from people obviously only semiliterate, and several were from those who had had no previous connection with the university.

[11] Board of Regents of the University of Oklahoma, "Minutes," November 7, 1945, 1932–33.

2.

ADA LOIS SIPUEL FISHER

I had no inkling about when a test application for the admission of a Negro would be filed with the university, but I suspected that it might be a short time before enrollment for the second semester of the 1945–46 school year, perhaps sometime in early January.

Actually, it was Monday, January 14, when a young Negro woman appeared at my office about eleven o'clock in the morning. She was accompanied by Roscoe Dunjee, of Oklahoma City, State President of the National Association for the Advancement of Colored People, and Dr. W. A. J. Bullock, of Chickasha, Regional Director of the association. The young woman was chic, charming, and well poised as she entered my office, and I remember thinking that the association had made an excellent choice of a student for the test case. Mr. Dunjee introduced her as Ada Lois Sipuel Fisher and told me that her home was in Chickasha. Mrs. Fisher was then seated in front of my desk, while Dunjee and Bullock occupied chairs on either side of her.

During the first few minutes of our visit Bullock and Mrs. Fisher said very little, obviously expecting Dunjee to lead the conversation. Dunjee was pleasant and very articulate in stating the reason for their visit. There was no hint of belligerence in his manner, only an apparent desire to accomplish a mission. He explained that Mrs. Fisher was the wife of Warren W. Fisher, whom she had married during her junior year at Langston University. She had graduated from Langston with honors and now wished to study law, which was not included in the curriculum at Langston, and for that reason she sought admission to the School of Law at the University of Oklahoma. She was aware that funds had been appropriated by the state legislature that would enable her to study law outside the state of Oklahoma, but she wished to attend an institution in her home state. During his presentation Dunjee turned occasionally to Mrs. Fisher for corroboration or amplification of statements he had made.

After Dunjee had completed these preliminary remarks, Mrs. Fisher said that she wished to enroll in the School of Law at the University of Oklahoma. She presented her transcript from Langston University and asked to be provided with forms to complete to apply for admission. I accepted her transcript and had it taken immediately to Roy Gittinger, Dean of Admissions, for evaluation.

While we were waiting for Dean Gittinger's report, I discussed with my visitors the provisions in the constitution and statutes of the state of Oklahoma that prohibited officers of the university from admitting a Negro to the institution. I explained that violation of the law on my part could be interpreted in court as a misdemeanor, punishable by a fine of not less than one hundred dollars a day. I emphasized that, while I was not in sympathy with the law, I certainly was not in a financial position to experiment with its enforcement.

My three visitors listened impassively to what I said. When I had finished, Dunjee assured me, with what seemed to be a tinge of amusement, that he and the others understood the law very well. They knew, he said, that I could not legally admit Mrs. Fisher to our School of Law or permit her to be admitted, but they hoped to receive a refusal of admission in writing that might be used as the basis for a court test—namely a refusal stating that she could not be admitted solely because of her race. He explained that refusal to admit her without giving race as the sole reason would handicap their efforts to gain relief through court action.

At about this point in our conversation a report came from Dean Gittinger that Mrs. Fisher was academically qualified for admission to the University of Oklahoma. I agreed to provide the letter Dunjee had requested and asked how the letter should be addressed, in view of the fact that the applicant's married name was Fisher, whereas the name on her transcript was Sipuel. Dunjee suggested, and Mrs. Fisher agreed, that the application was being made under her maiden name as on the transcript and that the letter refusing admission should be addressed to Ada Lois Sipuel. I called my secretary, and in the presence of my visitors dictated the following letter:

Dear Miss Sipuel:
This will acknowledge receipt of your application for admission to the Law School of the University of Oklahoma.

However, I must deny you admission to the University for the following reasons:

1. Title 70, Sections 452–464, inclusive, of the Oklahoma Statutes, 1941, prohibits colored students from attending the schools of Oklahoma, and makes it a misdemeanor for school officials to admit colored students to white schools, to instruct classes composed of mixed races, or to attend classes composed of mixed races.

2. The Board of Regents has specifically instructed the president of the University of Oklahoma to refuse admission to Negroes, giving as a basis of their decision the statutes of Oklahoma.

> Cordially yours,
> G. L. Cross, President

We continued our conversation while the letter was being typed, and I elaborated somewhat on the action the regents had taken in instructing me to refuse admission to Negroes. I assured my visitors that this action had been taken solely because of the law and not because of personal belief that education in Oklahoma should be offered on a basis of racial segregation.

In a few minutes my secretary returned with the letter ready for signature. I signed it and presented it, with an extra carbon copy, to Mrs. Fisher, who read it, folded it, and placed it in the envelope. Dunjee then expressed his satisfaction and his appreciation of the visit and letter, in which expression he was joined by Bullock and Miss Sipuel. The trio left my office and were taken to lunch by the members of the university's YMCA-YWCA Race Relations Committee.

I should add that included with the abundance of advice that I had received for use on such an occasion was the suggestion that, in the event a graduate of Langston appeared for admission to the university, refusal should be based on the fact that Langston was not an accredited institution, a maneuver that might reduce the prospect of successful court action. This suggestion, which had come from a high-ranking state political figure, seemed impractical because I knew that the university had permitted several white students to transfer from unaccredited institutions in the past. But, in reflecting on the events of the morning, I realized that Dunjee had expected I would follow that tactic.

The denial of admission was widely publicized in the state newspapers, and the day after Miss Sipuel's visit to my office there was an article in the *Oklahoma City Times* with the headline "Negro Student May Appeal O.U. Decision." The article stated that Miss Sipuel was expected to ask the Federal District Court for an order requiring Oklahoma University to admit her to the School of Law. It pointed out, erroneously, that the United States Supreme Court had decided that Missouri University should admit Lloyd Gaines, a Negro, to its law school. The article speculated that Oklahoma's position might be different, however, because the state legislature had made an annual appropriation of fifteen thousand dollars to pay the tuition of Negroes who found it necessary to leave the state for courses of study not available at Langston University.

A rumor was circulated early in February that Thurgood Marshall, the NAACP's chief counsel, would be in Oklahoma on February 15 to file a test suit and that he would be assisted by Amos Hall, a Negro attorney from

Tulsa. But it was not until April 6 that Hall, acting as attorney for Miss Sipuel, filed a petition for a writ of mandamus with Judge Ben T. Williams of the District Court of Cleveland County. The petition listed Ada Lois Sipuel as plaintiff and the Board of Regents of the University of Oklahoma, George L. Cross, Maurice H. Merrill, George Wadsack, and Roy Gittinger as defendants. Merrill was Acting Dean of the School of Law, Wadsack was Registrar of the University, and Gittinger was Dean of Admissions.

After reciting the facts of Miss Sipuel's application for admission to the School of Law and the subsequent refusal of admission with descriptions of the responsibilities of the various defendants in the affairs of the University, the petition ended with the following paragraph:

Therefore, plaintiff being otherwise remediless, prays this honorable court to issue a writ of mandamus requiring and compelling said defendants to comply with their statutory duty in the premises and admit the plaintiff in the School of Law of the said University of Oklahoma and have such other and further relief as may be just and proper.

Judge Williams took the petition under advisement for a few days and on April 9, 1946, issued an alternative writ of mandamus identical with the original, except for the ending, which had been changed to read as follows:[1]

Therefore, the court being fully advised in the premises find that an alternative writ of mandamus should be issued herein.

It is therefore ordered, considered and adjudged that all of the said defendants, Board of Regents of the University of

[1] No. 14807.

Oklahoma, George L. Cross, Maurice H. Merrill, George Wadsack and Roy Gittinger each and all of them, are hereby commanded that immediately after receipt of this writ, you admit into the School of Law of the said University of Oklahoma, the said plaintiff, Ada Lois Sipuel, or that you and each of you and all of you, the said defendants, appear before this court at ten o'clock A.M. on the twenty-sixth day of April, 1946, to show cause for your refusal so to do and that you then and there return this writ together with all proceedings thereof.

I had a strange feeling when my copy of the writ arrived and realized that I was a defendant in the first legal action designed to end segregation in Oklahoma's system of public education.

Arrangements were made for the office of the attorney general of Oklahoma to handle the case for the defendants. Fred Hansen, Assistant Attorney General, was given the responsibility of preparing the defense, and it was decided that Professors Merrill and John B. Cheadle, also of the School of Law, would assist him.

On April 23, Hansen asked for a continuance of the case to allow time for the preparation of a brief and memorandum explaining the state's position in the developing litigation. Hall agreed to the request, and Judge Williams granted a continuance to May 16. The request for a continuance may have been related to rumors that the State Board of Regents for Higher Education might establish a law school for Negroes as a part of the state's system of higher education. Substance appeared to be given to these rumors when the board, scheduled to meet on May 27, advanced the date of its meeting by two weeks, thus bringing the members into session before the day of the court hearing. However, the board apparently did little at the meeting other than discuss the cost of developing a school of law for Negroes.

As I recall, the date of the trial was subsequently reset at least twice, once by agreement of the attorneys involved and once by request of the plaintiff. Finally, on July 9, 1946, Judge Williams opened the hearing in the Cleveland County Courthouse shortly after 10:30 A.M. It was announced at the beginning of the trial that attorneys Hall and Hansen had agreed on a stipulation of facts, including the following: that the plaintiff desired to study law and the School of Law at the University of Oklahoma was the only law school in Oklahoma where she could receive such training, that the plaintiff had completed the full college course at Langston and possessed all the scholastic and moral qualifications required for admission to the university, and that she was denied admission solely because of her race and color.

During the morning Hall presented his arguments and asked for a writ of mandamus that would require the university to admit Miss Sipuel to the School of Law. He based his arguments on United States Supreme Court decisions involving similar cases from Maryland[2] and Missouri,[3] in which it had been ruled that the Fourteenth Amendment of the Constitution requires the states to furnish equal educational facilities for black and white races. The attorney for the defendants did not contend that equal educational opportunities for the two races were available in Oklahoma but based his defense on the state laws that made it a criminal offense for those in

[2] *Pearson* v. *Murray,* 169 Md. 478, 182A. 590 (1936).
[3] *Missouri* ex rel. *Gaines* v. *Canada,* 305 U.S. 337 (1938).

charge of an educational institution to permit mixing of the races in a classroom.

The court recessed at noon and reconvened at 2:00 P.M. Merrill concluded the case for the defense, and Hall gave his closing arguments for the plaintiff.

The large number of Negroes, students, and faculty members of the University of Oklahoma packed into the courtroom that day provided evidence of considerable interest in the case. All must have been impressed by the vigorous, yet apparently friendly arguments presented by the opposing lawyers.

The court recessed late in the afternoon and reconvened at 7:45 P.M. At that time Judge Williams ruled to deny the writ of mandamus on the basis that the laws of the state of Oklahoma prohibited the university from admitting Miss Sipuel. That evening Hall announced that he would appeal and would file a motion for a new trial within three days, the statutory requirement for an appeal. Hall filed a motion for a new trial on July 11, 1946, on the grounds that the court had made an error in denying the petition of the plaintiff for a writ of mandamus and that errors of law had occurred at the trial. Judge Williams overruled the motion on July 24, at which time the plaintiff gave notice in open court of her intention to appeal to the Oklahoma Supreme Court.

It is interesting to note that an apparent difference in the philosophies of Hall and Dunjee developed during the hearing and during interviews with the press following the hearing. Hall seemed to take the position that Miss Sipuel had been denied her rights under the separate-but-equal doctrine established by the decision of the United

43

States Supreme Court in the case of *Plessy* v. *Ferguson* (1895).[4] That case involved the constitutionality of a Louisiana statute requiring segregation on passenger vehicles. The petitioner had claimed that the statute was unconstitutional, a position that had not been sustained by the state courts. The Supreme Court affirmed the judgment of the Louisiana courts in holding that the statute in question did not violate either the Thirteenth or the Fourteenth amendment. Justice Henry B. Brown, in his opinion for the majority of the court, said:

> The statute which implies merely a legal distinction between the white and colored races—a distinction which is founded in the color of the two races, and which must always exist so long as white men are distinguished from the other race by color—has no tendency to destroy the legal equality of the two races, or re-establish a state of involuntary servitude.

But Dunjee made his contrasting position clear to the press from the beginning. He declared that there could be no separate-but-equal education—that equal opportunity could exist only where the same education was available to both races.

The Sipuel case was next appealed to the Oklahoma Supreme Court, and two new attorneys were named for the plaintiff, Marshall and Robert L. Carter. The attorneys for the plaintiff filed a motion for oral argument on January 24, 1947. The motion was granted, and oral argument was heard on March 4, 1947, when Marshall presented the plaintiff's case at the hearing and argued that segregation was a violation of the Fourteenth Amendment. Elaborating on the theme earlier pro-

---

[4] *Plessy* v. *Ferguson*, 163 U.S. 537 (1896).

pounded by Dunjee, Marshall urged that segregation in itself amounted to unlawful discrimination, that there could be no equality under a segregated system, and that such equality could be only "legal fiction" and "judicial myth."

But despite Marshall's impressive presentation, the Oklahoma Supreme Court, in an opinion filed on April 29, 1947, sustained the ruling of the Cleveland County District Court. In doing so, the court took the position that it was "the State Supreme Court's duty to maintain the State's policy of segregating white and Negro races for purposes of education so long as it does not conflict with the Federal Constitution." The court pointed out that it was the duty of the Board of Regents for Higher Education and the Board of Control for Langston University to provide Negroes with facilities for instruction equal to those enjoyed by white students at the University of Oklahoma but that the boards were entitled to reasonable advance notice of the intention of Negro students to require such facilities. The court also took the position that a Negro student who is a citizen and resident of Oklahoma has the same right as a white student to be educated in Oklahoma in preference to education in out-of-state schools with tuition aid from Oklahoma but that when the latter plan has been in operation for a number of years a Negro student preferring such education in the state should be required to make such preference definitely known to the proper authorities before the student could successfully claim unlawful discrimination and the lack of furnishing of educational facilities in Oklahoma.

Included in the opinion was this statement: "As we view the matter the state itself could place complete reliance upon the lack of a formal demand by petitioner." Apparently this statement was considered by the court to be in error because a correcting opinion was issued on June 15, 1947, by Chief Justice Thurman S. Hurst, amending it to read: "As we view the matter the state itself could not place complete reliance upon the lack of formal demand by the petitioner." Hurst's opinion continued:

We do not doubt it would be the duty of the state, without any formal demand, to provide equal educational facilities for the races, to the fullest extent indicated by any desired patronage, whether by formal demand or otherwise. But it does seem that before the state could be accused of discrimination for failure to institute a certain course of study for negroes, it should be shown there was some ready patronage therefor, or someone of the race desirous of such instruction.

A petition for a rehearing was filed by Miss Sipuel's attorneys on June 12. It was denied on June 24. The attorneys then filed with the United States Supreme Court a petition for a writ of certiorari on the grounds that the decisions of the Oklahoma courts had been inconsistent with the Supreme Court's ruling in the Gaines case.[5] The Court accepted the petition, and opposing arguments were heard on Thursday, January 8, 1948. The Court acted with startling, almost unprecedented, swiftness. According to the *New York Times* of January 13, 1948, a hint of the quick decision was given by ques-

[5] *Sipuel* v. *Board of Regents et al.*, "Petition for a Writ of Certiorari and Brief in support Thereof, United States Supreme Court, October Term, 1947 (copy in University of Oklahoma files).

tions that Justice Felix Frankfurter directed to the Oklahoma attorneys. Could Miss Sipuel be admitted to the university law school? Could a separate class be established for her in that school? Could she be admitted temporarily pending the establishment of a law school at Langston University? Could Langston University quickly set up a law school?

The Oklahoma lawyers, led by Assistant Attorney General Fred Hansen, responded that the State Regents for Higher Education had the power to do any of these things—an answer which might be considered questionable in part because the laws of the state at that time prohibited the regents from admitting Miss Sipuel to the university. At the end of the questioning Justice Robert H. Jackson observed dryly that a law school with one student would not provide "much of a law education."

On the following Monday, January 12, 1948, the Supreme Court issued its decision. It consisted of an unsigned, mimeographed, one-page document[6] ordering that Oklahoma must provide a legal education for the petitioner and provide it as soon as it would be provided for the applicants of any other racial group.

The order, seemingly based on the answers to Justice Frankfurter's questions—especially his question about whether Miss Sipuel could be admitted to the law school —obviously was intended to ensure that Miss Sipuel would be admitted immediately to the School of Law at the University of Oklahoma for second-semester classes, to begin on January 29. That was the interpretation of some members of the press, because the next day the

[6] See Appendix 1.

New York Times carried a story headlined "Supreme Court Orders Oklahoma to Admit a Negro to Law School." On the same day the *Daily Oklahoman* carried a front-page story with a half-inch headline: "Negro Law Student for O.U. in Prospect Under Court's Ruling." The *Oklahoma Daily*, the university paper, carried a large-type headline across the top of the front page: "Sipuel Wins Case!" The *Norman Transcript* of January 12, 1948, had headlined its front page, "High Court Orders University to Admit Negro Law Student." The *Oklahoma City Times* of January 12, 1948, had also used a more cautious headline: "Supreme Court Orders State to Provide Negro with Equal Legal Education Immediately." These interpretations were based on a consideration of the two alternatives open to the Oklahoma State Regents for Higher Education: admit Miss Sipuel to the School of Law at the University of Oklahoma or provide at once the same facilities at Langston University. Because the time factor appeared to preclude the possibility of immediately providing a law school at Langston, only the first alternative seemed available to the regents.

Miss Sipuel certainly believed that the decision meant that she could be admitted to the University of Oklahoma. She flew from Washington, D.C., to Oklahoma City on January 15. Her arrival at the Oklahoma City Municipal Airport was described as a "festive occasion" by Ray Parr, writing for the *Daily Oklahoman*. She was met at the airport by her mother, who lived in Chickasha, a committee from the state branch of the NAACP, and several photographers, who greeted her as she stepped from the airplane.

Her husband, who had appeared with her for the first time in Washington, D.C., and was expected to accompany her to Oklahoma, was not with her; he had decided instead to return to Providence, Rhode Island, where he was employed as a machinist. His appearance in Washington came as a distinct surprise to the attorneys for the defendants, who, owing to an oversight on my part, had not realized that she was married. When it became known that she had a husband, her married name was used thereafter in the newspapers and in subsequent court action.

In the interview that followed her landing at the Oklahoma City airport, Mrs. Fisher was quoted by Ray Parr as saying, "Oh, it's a wonderful constitution . . . . I'm going to be a lawyer. I'm going to learn." She went on to say that she did not think she would be "alone for long" at the University of Oklahoma. "Somebody had to be first; it will be hard but maybe soon there'll be other Negroes with me."

According to Parr, she said that she had decided to make her present fight for admission to the University of Oklahoma while she was a junior at Langston. Her decision was influenced, she said, by a state official who, when asked for better facilities for Langston, "just shrugged his shoulders and said we were lucky to have any school." She went on to say: "Six of us decided to apply for various departments at the University of Oklahoma. Everybody backed out, so I nominated myself chief guinea pig." She said that she did not plan to live on the campus, that she was interested only in learning, not socializing. She did say that she hoped, if admitted, to make friends with her fellow students and then added, somewhat forebodingly, "The few on the campus who might call me names—why, I won't even hear them."

But her triumph was short-lived. Attorney General Mac Q. Williamson came forth almost immediately with the opinion that the Supreme Court's decision did not invalidate the segregation laws of Oklahoma, and on January 17 the state supreme court, to which the case had been remanded, entered an order as follows:

Said Board of Regents is hereby directed, under the authority conferred upon it by the provisions of Art. 13-A, Constitution of the State of Oklahoma, and Title 70 O.S. 1941, Secs. 1976, 1979, to afford to plaintiff, and all others similarly situated, an opportunity, in conformity with the equal protection clause of the Fourteenth Amendment of the Federal Constitution and with the provisions of the Constitution and statutes of this state requiring segregation of the races in the schools of this state. Art. 13, Sec. 3, Constitution of Oklahoma; 70 O.S. 1941, Secs. 451-457.

Reversed with directions to the trial court to take such proceedings as may be necessary to fully carry out the opinion of the Supreme Court of the United States and this opinion. The mandate is ordered to issue forthwith.

The ruling implied, although it did not say so specifically, that Mrs. Fisher should not be permitted to enter the University of Oklahoma School of Law at the beginning of the second semester, which was to open on January 29.

When Chancellor M. A. Nash, Executive Officer of the Oklahoma State Regents for Higher Education, received the decision of the state supreme court, he announced that a meeting of the state regents would be held on Monday, January 19, to "wrestle with the problem."

Without waiting for action by the regents, Mrs. Fisher appeared at the registrar's office of the University of Oklahoma at 11:00 A.M. on January 19 and asked John E. Fellows, who had succeeded Roy Gittinger as Dean of Admissions and Records, for admission to the university. Dean Fellows gave her an application for admission, which she filled out and left in his office. The dean told her, however, that no action could be taken on her application until word had been received from the state regents about how the case should be handled.

The confusing situation could have been avoided had the United States Supreme Court faced its responsibilities squarely when the case was presented on January 8. An editorial expressing this view appeared in the *New York Times* on January 15:

> In its forthright order to the State of Oklahoma to provide legal education for a young Negro woman, the Supreme Court reaffirmed its eight-year-old decision that educational privileges cannot be denied any qualified applicant on artificial grounds of race or color. So far, so good. But not far enough. The Court again begged the issue as to whether state's segregation laws are constitutional, whether establishment by Oklahoma of a School of Law for Negroes or others, comparable in faculty and facilities to that provided for white students, meets the tests of constitutionality under the Fourteenth Amendment. . . . Equal facilities for Negroes separate from those for other races would seem to be an impossibility. The very fact of segregation makes them unequal.

The final paragraph laid the issue squarely on the line:

If the United States is to stand before the world as an exemplar of equality of rights, if it is to urge with integrity the acceptance by the rest of the world of the tenets and practices of a democratic society, then it would be well if we set our own records straight. It seems to us that the language of the Fourteenth Amendment must be tortured out of common meaning to make segregation practices in education anything except unconstitutional.

The State Regents for Higher Education met on Monday, January 19, as Chancellor Nash had announced. At their meeting, after what must have been much painful soul-searching, they established by resolution the "Langston University School of Law, which school shall be located in Oklahoma City, Oklahoma County, Oklahoma." Responsibility for putting the newly established school into operation was left to a committee of five regents: John Rogers, of Tulsa; Frank Buttram, of Oklahoma City; W. D. Little, of Ada; Dial Curran, of Shawnee; and Guy M. Harris, of Ardmore. This committee, with the cooperation of the Regents for the Agricultural and Mechanical Colleges (the governing board for Langston University) was faced with the almost impossible problem of creating the new school and getting it into operation by the time students would be enrolling at the University of Oklahoma Law School for the second semester on the Norman campus—just one week later.

In the meantime, the highly controversial case had been remanded to the Cleveland County District Court to be placed on record and a new journal entry issued— an entry that would conform with the opinion of the United States Supreme Court and the recent order of the state supreme court. The case came before the district court on Thursday, January 22, when Judge Hinshaw heard arguments presented by the opposing lawyers concerning the exact meanings of the decisions of the appellate courts.

Hall, attorney for the plaintiff, asked the district judge to issue an immediate order admitting Mrs. Fisher to the School of Law on the grounds that the newly created School of Law for Negroes was not equal in quality to the School of Law at the University of Oklahoma. Judge Hinshaw refused to issue the order and also refused to rule on Hall's contention concerning the quality of the new Negro law school because, he said, the question was not before the court at that time, there having been no testimony about facilities provided by the new school.[7]

Strenuous effort had been made that week to develop the new School of Law of Langston University. It was decided that Rooms 426, 427, and 428 at the state capitol and the Oklahoma State Library would comprise the facilities of the new school. After consultation with W. Page Keeton, Dean of the School of Law at the University of Oklahoma, R. T. Stuart, Chairman of the Board of Regents for Agricultural and Mechanical Colleges, announced the appointment of a faculty of three who would serve the new school. Jerome E. Hemry, a forty-two-year-old attorney in Oklahoma City, was appointed dean at a salary of six thousand dollars a year. Randell S. Cobb, former Attorney General of the State of Oklahoma, was appointed Professor of Law at five thousand dollars a year, and Arthur Ellsworth, a thirty-year-old

[7] See Appendix 2.

attorney from Oklahoma City, was appointed professor at forty-five hundred dollars a year.

When the faculty for the new School of Law for Negroes had been completed on January 24, the State Regents for Higher Education proclaimed (with what must have been tongue in cheek) that a separate school of law had been established in Oklahoma City for Negroes that was "substantially equal in every way to the University Law School." G. L. Harrison, President of Langston University, announced the opening of the Langston University School of Law as follows: "Enrollment dates have been set for January 26, 27, and 28. Applicants are asked to report between the hours of 8:00 A.M. and 5:00 P.M., January 26, 27 or 28, Room 428, State Capitol Building for further information." President Harrison added, "Available for the new law school is the Oklahoma State Library, which contains one of the best law libraries in the entire southwest." Then, with what turned out to be unwarranted optimism, he allegedly said that it was his belief that Langston University School of Law would be a substantial answer to a need in the state. He later denied that he had made the statement after receiving several phone calls of protest from Negroes throughout the state.

I had received a letter from the office of the State Regents for Higher Education telling of the new "substantially equal" School of Law for Negroes with the suggestion that Mrs. Fisher not be admitted to the School of Law at the University of Oklahoma. The regents of the university previously had passed a resolution instructing the university to deny enrollment to Mrs. Fisher if the state regents ruled that the Oklahoma City school was "substantially equal." When I reported to the president of the university regents that I had received the certifying letter from the office of the state regents, I was instructed to obtain additional confirmation by telegram from the state regents' office before refusing admission to Mrs. Fisher.

To the surprise of practically no one on the Norman campus, Mrs. Fisher and her attorneys would have no part of the new law school. She said flatly that she would not enroll, and her attorneys announced that they would renew their efforts to have her admitted to the School of Law at the University of Oklahoma.

Enrollment day for the second semester of the school year arrived on Monday, January 26, before I had received confirmation by telegram of the new school's equality. I had a feeling that it would be difficult to know what to do when Mrs. Fisher appeared to apply for admission that morning, as I was quite sure she would. I carefully studied the resolution that had been passed by the Board, and found it provided for denial of admission if (1) confirmation of the existence of a Negro law school substantially equal in quality to the one at the University had been obtained from the Regents for Higher Education; (2) I had received a written opinion from the attorney general of the state, stating that Mrs. Fisher should not be admitted; or (3) the District Court of Cleveland County had refused to issue a writ of mandamus to Mrs. Fisher.

I was in the process of reflecting that I was not clear with respect to any of these points when Mrs. Fisher came to Dean John Fellows' office at about 10:30 that morning. With her were J. A. Cox, Jr., a member of the Oklahoma City branch of the NAACP; William S. Boyd, of El Reno, a regional NAACP official; and a reporter from the *Black Dispatch*. Not knowing what to do, Dean Fellows brought the group to my office, where I was regretfully forced to report that I did not know what to do either but that I would call Attorney General Mac Q. Williamson and ask for instructions.

I was able to get the attorney general on the telephone, but he was cautiously noncommittal in his responses to my questions. I then placed a call to Chancellor Nash, who was meeting with the state regents that day at Edmond. The call could not be completed immediately, and so I told Mrs. Fisher that as soon as I had talked with Chancellor Nash I would notify her by telephone whether she could be admitted. Exhibiting great patience, she left my office to return to Oklahoma City. Later in the day I received a telegram from Chancellor Nash confirming that the new Negro law school was substantially equal in quality to the one at the university. I was then able to inform Mrs. Fisher that she could not be admitted, and I released the information to the press.

That evening the *Norman Transcript* carried the headlines "O.U. Bans Negro Girl Again; New U.S. Court Action Asked." The latter portion of the headline referred to the fact that Mrs. Fisher's attorneys had anticipated the rejection of her application and, when this was confirmed, had filed that day a petition asking the United States Supreme Court to order Oklahoma officials to admit her "forthwith" to the University of Oklahoma

Mrs. Ada Lois Sipuel Fisher, photographed on January 14, 1946, the day she applied for admission to the University of Oklahoma. Courtesy *Oklahoman and Times.*

57

Mrs. Fisher applied for and was denied admission to the University of Oklahoma on January 14, 1946. On the left is Dr. W. A. J. Bullock, Chickasha physician and regional director of the National Association for the Advancement of Colored People. On the right is Roscoe Dunjee. Courtesy *Oklahoman and Times.*

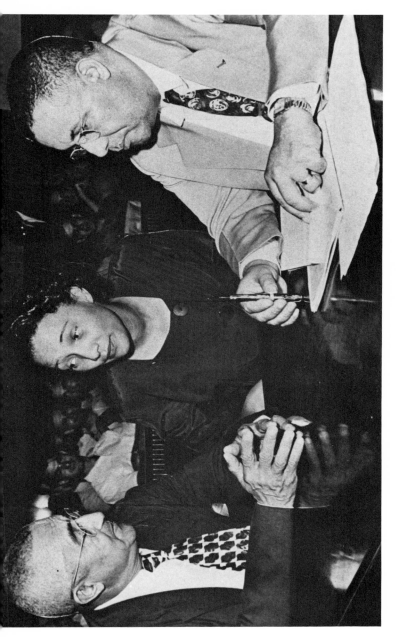

Mrs. Fisher confers with Dunjee (left) and her attorney, Amos T. Hall, of Tulsa, during the first court session in July, 1946. Courtesy *Oklahoman and Times*.

Mrs. Fisher and her husband, Warren W. Fisher, on January 12, 1948, after the United States Supreme Court ordered the state of Oklahoma to provide facilities for her to study law. Courtesy *Oklahoman and Times.*

Mrs. Fisher greeted by her mother, Mrs. M. B. Sipuel, of Chickasha, when she returned to Oklahoma following the Supreme Court decision. Courtesy *Oklahoman and Times.*

Mrs. Fisher reapplied for admission to the University of Oklahoma on January 19, 1948. With her, left to right: Amos T. Hall, resident counsel for the NAACP; Thurgood Marshall, attorney from the New York office of the NAACP; and Dr. H. W. Williamston, Idabel, state president of the NAACP. Courtesy *Oklahoman and Times.*

Jerome E. Hemry, dean of the newly established Langston University School of Law and an Oklahoma City attorney, attaches a sign to the door of room 428 in the State Capitol Building, Oklahoma City, January 25, 1948. With him are Arthur Ellsworth (center) and Randall S. Cobb. Courtesy *Oklahoman and Times.*

Mrs. Fisher and her attorneys, Thurgood Marshall and Amos Hall (standing, left to right), discuss enrollment with John E. Fellows (left), dean of admissions of the university, January 30, 1948. Courtesy *Oklahoman and Times*.

Mrs. Fisher entering the University of Oklahoma School of Law, June, 1949. Courtesy Office of Media Information, University of Oklahoma.

School of Law. But the Court was in recess at the time and was not scheduled to return to the bench until February 2.

In the meantime, other developments added to the confusion of the situation. Wednesday, January 28, was the last day of enrollment for the second semester of the school year. During that morning I received a telephone call telling me that six Negroes wished to apply that day for admission to the University of Oklahoma to pursue courses of study not available to members of their race at a Negro university in Oklahoma. I cannot recall who placed the call, but the caller asked for an appointment to discuss the matter with me during the afternoon. I agreed to meet the new applicants at 2:00 P.M.

Included in the group asking for admission were Mozell A. Dillon, a graduate of Langston University who wanted to do graduate work in architectural engineering; Helen M. Holmes, a graduate of Lincoln University at Jefferson City, Missouri, who wished to study commercial education at the graduate level; Ivor Tatum, a graduate in social work from Kansas University; Mrs. Mauderie Hancock Wilson, a graduate of Langston, who wished to study social work at the graduate level; George W. McLaurin, a graduate with a master's degree from Kansas University and a member of the Langston faculty, who wanted to work for a doctorate in education; and James Bond, a member of the Langston faculty who wished to pursue a program of study leading to a doctoral degree in zoology.

The six applicants were accompanied by James A. Giddings, a member of the NAACP. However, both

Giddings and the group denied that they were being sponsored in any way by the NAACP, and Giddings emphasized that he was not representing the organization.

Also with the group was Malcomb Whitby, a Negro reporter for the *Black Dispatch*. His presence in my office was protested by other reporters who had come to the Administration Building looking for stories, and I asked Whitby if he would mind waiting with the other reporters until I had completed the conference with the applicants and could be free to hold a press conference. Whitby graciously agreed to leave the office.

The significance of the several applications was plain and was freely discussed by the applicants. They were relying on the decision of the United States Supreme Court in the Fisher case, which stipulated that the state of Oklahoma must provide a legal education for Mrs. Fisher and "provide it as soon as it does for applicants of any other group." The six applicants, appearing as they did on the afternoon of the final day of enrollment, had reasoned that the Supreme Court's decision would cover their applications for admission to the university, and that, under the decision, they must be admitted or new programs in their various fields of interests would have to be established for Negroes in the state. The alternative would be to deny enrollment to all others in these fields. Although the State Regents for Higher Education had performed something of a miracle in organizing a new law school for Negroes in less than a week's time, the applicants that day thought there was little chance that the new programs they sought could be provided overnight.

It appeared to me that the ruling of the Supreme Court did indeed cover their cases, but, remembering the state laws and the daily fine that I might incur if I admitted them, I had little inclination to experiment in this new desegregation development. I told the group that I could not admit them without conferring with the regents of the university and possibly the state regents but that I would have an answer for them as soon as possible—and that, in their cases, the deadline for admission would be extended.

As soon as the applicants left my office, I placed a phone call to Lloyd Noble, of Ardmore, President of the Board of Regents of the University of Oklahoma, and told him what had happened. He asked that a meeting of the university regents be called for the next morning, Thursday, January 29, at 10:00 A.M. He indicated that he would get in touch with the office of the state regents and expressed the belief that that board would also want to meet. I then called the chancellor of the State Regents and asked him to provide immediate certification whether educational facilities in the graduate fields involved in the six applications were available to Negroes elsewhere in Oklahoma so that the regents of the university would have at least some information upon which to base their discussion.

The university regents assembled for their meeting in the Administration Building a little before 10:00 A.M. on Thursday. An interesting prelude to their session occurred when another group met an hour earlier on Parrington Oval just north of the Administration Building, between the old Carnegie Library Building and

Old Science Hall. There a crowd of approximately one thousand students and faculty (by estimate of the campus police) assembled to protest the denial of admission of Negroes to the University of Oklahoma. The demonstration, according to newspaper accounts, had been initiated by Howard Friedman, a student from Oklahoma City.

At the protest meeting Friedman spoke briefly against the injustice of segregated education and, according to an article in the *Oklahoma City Times* that afternoon, wound up his remarks with the following:

> You and I have an obligation to protect the Negro students and any other minority group. Second-class citizenship cannot exist. This is an extension of the Hitler myth. We thought we did away with it. Let it be known that O.U. is receptive to equal education. We are not hypocrites. Draw up petitions and send them to the Regents.

His remarks were cheered loudly by those who had assembled in the oval and by students and faculty of the School of Home Economics and the College of Education who were watching from the windows of Old Science Hall and the Carnegie Building.

Following Friedman's remarks Wanda Lou Howard, of Marlowe, Oklahoma, and Jack Bales, of Dewey, spoke briefly. The demonstration ended with the burning of a copy of the Fourteenth Amendment. The copy was torn to shreds by Friedman and placed in a cookie can held by Miss Howard. The pieces were then doused with lighter fluid and ignited by Bales. When the flames had died down and the ashes cooled, the remains were placed in an envelope addressed to President Harry S Truman. Then a portion of the crowd, singing "The Battle Hymn of the Republic," marched to the campus corner post-office, where the letter was mailed. The entire demonstration lasted only about fifteen minutes, possibly shortened because of the fifteen-degree weather and the three or four inches of snow covering the campus.

During the morning the State Regents for Higher Education met and referred the question of the enrollment of the six Negroes to Attorney General Williamson. Williamson, who had been alerted the preceding evening, later reported that he had worked all of Wednesday night preparing an opinion, which was submitted to the university regents the next day. The salient point in the opinion was that "the Board of Regents would be justified in declining the admission [of the six applicants] at this time."

After struggling with their dilemma for most of Thursday, the regents adopted a resolution requesting the attorney general to give a more positive ruling about whether the regents might lawfully admit qualified Negroes when other equal facilities were not available. They also asked me to secure written certification from Chancellor Nash about whether the programs sought by the six Negro applicants were available for Negroes in any other institutions supported and maintained by the taxpayers of Oklahoma. I had received oral assurance from the chancellor's office that such programs were not available, but the regents wanted it in writing. They ended their day's work by instructing me to secure such certification and then follow the ruling of the attorney general, when it was forthcoming, in handling the applications.

Over an article by Ray Parr, the headlines the next morning, Friday, January 30, 1948, were: "Negro Question Is Tossed Back to Williamson; The University Regents Demand Attorney Say 'Yes' or 'No' Plainly." It occurred to me that this was a fair summarization of Thursday's efforts.

The anti-Negro segments of the campus and community made their views known that morning through a mass meeting held just north of the Administration Building. A crowd of approximately 350 assembled to protest the admission of Negroes to the university. The meeting lasted about three-quarters of an hour, during which time several speakers argued the issue noisily over a loudspeaker system with intermittent interruptions by hecklers. At the close of the meeting the organizers presented me with a petition signed by 282 of their fellow segregationists, asking that Negroes not be admitted to the university.

A third demonstration was held on the north side of the Administration Building on Saturday morning, but its purpose was to spotlight the futility of demonstrations. Clee Fitzgerald, a freshman law student from Caddo, Oklahoma, presided and presented several speakers to an audience of about one hundred persons. The theme of the meeting was "equality for the Irish," and many of the participants wore green armbands. The list of speakers included Ferrill Rogers, a senior law student from Stillwater, and Tom Brett, another law senior from Ardmore. They presented strong pleas for equal rights for the Irish and asked for recognition in Oklahoma of the "Railroad Act of 1842, which assured Irishmen of certain rights in laying railroad ties." A copy of the "act" was burned and mailed to the head janitor of the Student Union Building.[8]

On the whole, the issue of desegregation did not cause any great excitement within the university student body or faculty. The great majority of the approximately twelve thousand students on the campus went about their business quietly and with little apparent interest in the problem. I have never doubted that Negroes could have been admitted to the institution at the time without serious protest. The problems we were experiencing were a result of the segregation laws of the state and the failure of the United States Supreme Court to face the issue squarely in handling the Fisher case. The court's evasive ruling in this case was in great contrast to future rulings from the same source during the next two decades.

The attorney general worked on the problem during Friday and Saturday. Late Saturday he announced to the press that the university regents would not be justified in admitting the six Negroes for graduate studies. I was busy with calls from reporters that evening, but could tell them only that the six applicants probably would be notified Monday that they could not be admitted legally to the university. However, I qualified my statement by saying that I would wait until I had seen a copy of the attorney general's ruling. The ruling was received Mon-

---

[8] Larry Stephenson, "The Sipuel Case," *Sooner Magazine*, January, 1948, 5.

day, and the notifications of denial were sent to the six applicants that day.

In the meantime, John Rogers, a member of the State Regents for Higher Education and a prominent Tulsa attorney, became the first public figure to suggest that the state laws should be modified to permit Negroes to enter graduate schools in Oklahoma. He was quoted by Ray Parr in the January 29 issue of the *Daily Oklahoman* as saying that such a course would be more "economic and feasible" than to attempt to provide equal opportunities under the law through the establishment of a graduate school exclusively for Negroes.

An interesting new confusion was injected into the situation on Friday, January 31, when Walter M. Harrison, a white man and well-known former managing editor of the *Daily Oklahoman* and *Oklahoma City Times*, applied for admission to the new School of Law for Negroes in Oklahoma City. Harrison insisted that his application was made in good faith; he wanted to study law there because he and his family lived in Oklahoma City. At first his application was refused by Dean Hemry, but later it was announced that a decision concerning the matter would be delayed. The decision apparently was complicated by the fact that no Negro students had enrolled in the new law school, and consequently Harrison's attendance would not be in violation of the state laws.

Harrison was a very interesting person. Energetic and brilliant, in later years he was to write a book involved with the history of Oklahoma entitled *Me and My Big Mouth* (1954). He did not enter the Oklahoma City branch of Langston University to study law because Dean Hemry finally announced that the school was for Negroes only and that Harrison could not be admitted unless he signed a statement saying that he was of Negro blood. I believe that no formal action was ever taken on his application, however.

An interesting by-product of the Fisher case was the decision of the University of Arkansas, announced by President Lewis W. Jones, that a Negro student would be admitted as a result of the United States Supreme Court's decision in the Fisher case.[9] However, Arkansas, like Oklahoma, was plagued by segregation laws, and, in order to comply with these laws, the student, Clifford Davis, was provided with a separate classroom where he would be given the same courses and would hear the same lectures by the same faculty members as the white students. This arrangement foreshadowed what was to happen at the University of Oklahoma within a very short time.

During the next couple of weeks I spent much time speculating about what legal action might be taken by the NAACP or by the six Negroes. I pondered also what the Supreme Court might do with Mrs. Fisher's petition for a writ of mandamus to compel compliance with the Court's mandate of January 12, 1948, when the Court resumed its activities early in February. The answer to the latter question was forthcoming on February 16, 1948, when the high court denied Mrs. Fisher's petition for a writ of mandamus. In giving its per curiam opinion (No. 325), the Court declared:

[9] *Daily Oklahoman* (Oklahoma City), January 31, 1948.

It is clear that the District Court of Cleveland County did not depart from our mandate . . . Nothing which may have transpired since the orders of the Oklahoma courts were issued is in the record before us, nor could we consider it on this petition for a writ of mandamus if it were. The Oklahoma District Court has retained jurisdiction to hear and determine any question arising under its order. Whether or not the order is followed or disobeyed should be determined by it in the first instance. The manner in which, or the method by which, Oklahoma may have satisfied, or could satisfy, the requirements of the mandate of this Court, as applied by the District Court of Cleveland County in its order of January 22, 1948, is not before us.

Motion for leave to file petition for writ of mandamus is denied.

The opinion was given without oral argument. One member of the Supreme Court, Justice Frank Murphy, expressed his belief that a hearing should have been held to determine whether the actions of the Oklahoma courts subsequent to the issuance of the Supreme Court's mandate might constitute an evasion of that mandate. Another member, Justice Wiley B. Rutledge, dissented from the opinion.[10]

Political figures of the state for the most part had steered clear of the controversy. However, there had been some commentary following Mrs. Fisher's original application for admission to the university. Fred McDuff, a possible Democratic candidate for governor from Seminole, Oklahoma, made what the newspapers interpreted as an effort to inject the issue into the 1946 political campaign. Early in February he was quoted as

10 See Appendix 3.

74

criticizing "those backing the attempt to secure the girl's enrollment." He apparently was referring to Dunjee, who had lashed out editorially about educational facilities for Negroes in Oklahoma. In the newspaper articles McDuff was reported as favoring the expansion of Langston University and the creation of another Negro college in the Muskogee area. He allegedly stated that he believed Negroes preferred to have their own educational facilities rather than to have to force themselves into white colleges and universities.

But after the six additional Negroes filed applications for admission, there was talk in political circles of the need to call a special session of the legislature to cope with the problem. State Representative Harold Carey of Oklahoma City was reported in the February 1, 1948, issue of the *Norman Transcript* as saying that he would spearhead the organization of a special session if Governor Roy Turner failed to call one.

Until that time Governor Turner had maintained a hands-off policy, but, apparently stimulated by telegrams and other communications he received following the multiple applications, he announced to the newspapers that during the week he would be in touch with various state agencies and officials involved in the Negroes' fight for admission to graduate study at the university.

As a result of Governor Turner's interest and discussions with the state regents, the board organized a committee of six deans, three from the University of Oklahoma and three from Oklahoma A&M College, to study and make recommendations concerning the best means of solving Oklahoma's problems of equal educational facilities for Negroes. Chancellor Nash served as chairman of the committee. The University of Oklahoma was represented on the committee by Deans Arnold Joyal, Laurence Snyder, and Edgar D. Meacham.

The committee, through its chairman, reported back to the board on Monday, March 23, 1948. The principal item of the report was the recommendation that Negroes be admitted to the University of Oklahoma and to Oklahoma A&M College for graduate and advanced professional programs. The deans advised against any attempt to develop graduate and professional programs at Langston University on the grounds that such might jeopardize the recently acquired accreditation of Langston by the North Central Association of Colleges and Universities.

The committee reported that it would cost between ten and twelve million dollars to provide physical facilities for graduate work at Langston and that, even if such funds could become available, four or five years would be required to construct the facilities. Moreover, an additional annual budget of about five hundred thousand dollars would be needed for operations. The committee predicted that, even if these sums were spent in the development of Langston University, no more than twenty-five or thirty Negroes would enroll in the new courses during a school year. However, the committee did recommend that,

when Langston University makes the request, with approval of the North Central Association, graduate courses be offered in education, social work, home economics, and music at the institution; that the plan of giving financial aid to Negroes attending institutions in other states be made more liberal; that Oklahoma continue to cooperate in the present consideration being given regional plans for higher education; and that the president, faculty and authorities responsible for accreditation of Langston be commended and that the effort to strengthen the Negro university program be continued.

The committee's report caused something of a stir throughout the state. To carry out the recommendations would mean a special session of the legislature or a dangerous delay in action until that legislative body convened in January, 1949. Several political leaders predicted that the legislature would not repeal the segregation laws if it were called into session.[11]

During the latter part of February, Governor Turner took other action that I think was related directly or indirectly to the desegregation movement. He telephoned me one day and told me something of the activities of the Southern Governors' Council. The governors, concerned about the increasing need for specialized educational facilities in the South, were considering a proposal whereby southern states might cooperatively establish specialized educational facilities for Negroes in all fields and also establish regional specialized schools for white students—schools of veterinary science, medicine, and so on. He mentioned that the state of Florida did not have a publicly supported school of medicine and that Oklahoma had no programs in dentistry and veterinary science. He asked me to represent him at a meeting of the Southern Governors' Conference, scheduled to be

[11] *Daily Oklahoman*, March 23, 1948.

held at Gainesville, Florida, over a three-day period during the first week of March. He told me that Henry J. Bennett, President of Oklahoma A&M College, would also be attending the meeting. He said that a proposal for regional educational centers would come up for discussion at the meeting, and he hoped that I would be able to evaluate the proposal for him when I returned. It immediately occurred to me that the proposal probably represented a cooperative effort on the part of the southern states to meet the growing threat of legal action against their segregation laws, and although I had little sympathy with this idea, I did agree to represent the governor at the conference.

I roomed with President Bennett in a Gainesville hotel during the conference, and I found him to be one of the most genial and engaging personalities that I had ever met. I was especially impressed by the way he maintained frequent contact with his institution at Stillwater. He carried a copy of the school's budget in his briefcase and telephoned the personnel in his office two or three times a day. This temporarily caused me to distrust my own administrative policy of instructing the people in my office not to call me when I was on a trip except in case of emergency.

Discussions at the three-day conference were interesting and very productive. I found, as I had suspected, that many of the participants were interested in using the plan for regional centers as a means of providing "segregated but equal" educational facilities for Negroes, but a substantial number of the participants seemed genuinely interested in the broader possibilities for co-

operation the plan offered, especially the development
of very expensive laboratories for research in nuclear and
other sciences. From discussions at the meeting there
emerged a plan for the organization of the Southern
Regional Educational Compact Commission, which later
developed cooperative effort on the part of member institutions. The Oak Ridge Institute for Nuclear Studies was
one result.

Worthy of note at this time is an address which Dean
Laurence H. Snyder made on the campus of the University of Oklahoma late in February, following the denial
of admission to the six Negro students. Dean Snyder had
been induced to leave Ohio State University and accept
the deanship of the Graduate School at the University of
Oklahoma, effective in September, 1947. He was already
enjoying a distinguished career at the time he made the
transfer. A pioneer student in human genetics who had
received much credit for opening the field in the United
States, Dean Snyder was the author of four textbooks
dealing with genetics and sixty or more articles published in scientific journals. He was an effective, much-
sought-after public speaker whose remarks always had a
very positive impact on his audience.

On the occasion mentioned above, while discussing
the responsibility of state universities, he declared: "If
universities, which are supposedly the epitome of culture
and learning in our society, cannot practice the principles of democracy and illustrate them by example, where
in the world will they be illustrated and practiced?" He
made this remark in relation to the segregation laws of
Oklahoma and the litigation they had precipitated. *Time*

magazine was sufficiently impressed by the above remark to quote it in the March 8, 1948 issue and to add
additionally that Dean Snyder hoped that "in the very
near future the Graduate College [at the University of
Oklahoma] would be open to every intellectually qualified Oklahoman whatever his race." *Time* added, quite
accurately, that Dean Snyder's audience, which included
two hundred faculty members, applauded in approval.

On March 15, 1948, Mrs. Fisher entered the picture
once again when her attorney, Hall, filed a motion (original case No. 14807) in the District Court of Cleveland
County, which contended that the Langston University
School of Law did not afford advantages for legal education to Negro students "substantially equal" to those
afforded to white students at the School of Law of the
University of Oklahoma and that for this reason she was
entitled to be admitted at once to the School of Law at
the University of Oklahoma. The motion stated further
that the petitioner would offer to support her contention
"by oral testimony, documents and other evidence."

The district court set April 5, 1948, as the date for the
hearing of the motion. But there were delays, and the
hearing finally was held on May 24 through 27, inclusive.
Thurgood Marshall and Amos Hall appeared in court as
attorneys for the plaintiff.

Among an imposing group of witnesses assembled for
the hearing were Max Radin, Professor of Law at the
University of California; Charles Bunn, Chairman of the
Curriculum Committee of the University of Wisconsin;
Erwin N. Griswold, Dean of the Harvard Law School;
Earl G. Harrison, Dean of the University of Pennsylvania

Law School; Walter Gellhorn, Professor of Law at Columbia University; John G. Hervey, former Dean of the
University of Oklahoma Law School; Page Keeton, Dean
of the Law School of the University of Oklahoma; and
Henry H. Foster, Jr., former attorney with the National
Labor Relations Board and a member of the law faculty
of the University of Oklahoma.

After the preliminaries were disposed of, Dean Keeton
testified that he did not believe that opportunities at the
Langston Law School would be equal to those at the law
school at the state university. He added, however, that
he did not want to attempt to judge a school that was not
in operation. He thought that the physical plant of the
Langston institution might be satisfactory but that the
serious weakness would be the lack of a substantial number of faculty members whose principal interest would
be that of teaching. He said also that he preferred larger
classes than would be possible in the new institution.[12]

Professor Foster then testified, startling the court with
the vigor of his testimony and charging state officials
with "cheap political chicanery." He branded the Langston School of Law a "fake, fraud and deception."[13]
When asked whether two law schools with the character-
istics of those under discussion could afford equal educational opportunities for students, Foster shouted, "Only a
prejudiced or an academic mind could conceivably find
the slightest substance to say that the two schools are at
all comparable, let alone substantially equal or equivalent." According to Ray Parr, writing for the May 24

[12] *Ibid.*, May 25, 1948.
[13] *Oklahoma City Times*, May 25, 1948.

81

edition of the *Daily Oklahoman*, Foster went on to say, "It is a fake, it is a fraud, it is a deception. It is to my mind an attempt to avoid the clear-cut mandate of the United States Supreme Court. I think it is indecent." According to Parr's story, when questioned by Attorney General Williamson concerning the responsibility of public officials to uphold the laws of the state after taking oaths, Foster replied, "I think the Attorney General should start now to uphold the Constitution of the United States which he has been ignoring the past six months in violation of his oath of office."

At the conclusion of Williamson's questioning, Judge Hinshaw, perhaps somewhat shaken by Foster's forceful outburst, declared a five-minute recess as Foster left the stand—possibly to give the court time to regain its composure.

During the remaining days of the hearing the court heard testimony from former Dean Hervey and the five distinguished people who had come from beyond the state's borders to testify.

Hervey, at that time legal adviser to the Council on Legal Education and Admissions of the American Bar Association, was the principal witness for the state. He testified that in his opinion a student could obtain a legal education at the Langston University law school that would be equivalent to the one available at the University of Oklahoma. He stressed the superiority—both in materials and in reading quarters—of the state law library in Oklahoma City over the university law school library in Norman. He praised the faculty of the new law school and suggested that there were definite advantages to having small classes. The proximity of the new school to the state supreme court was claimed also as a distinct advantage. He went on to say that, considering the ratio of faculty members to students, the Langston faculty should be rated superior to the faculty of the university in its capacity to provide a legal education. At the university there were eleven faculty members for 552 students; at Langston the ratio would be four to one.

But the five out-of-state witnesses strongly disagreed with Hervey. Radin, Bunn, Griswold, Harrison, and Gellhorn all emphasized the importance of a substantial student body in modern methods of teaching law. Harrison testified that legal opportunities would be "infinitely superior" at the University of Oklahoma; Langston could not properly be called a law school. Griswold emphatically stated that the two schools were "not equal, not substantially equal, not so nearly that there is any fair basis for comparison."

After four days of hearing conflicting testimony concerning the quality of the two law schools, Judge Hinshaw said that he would take Mrs. Fisher's case under advisement and make a decision in two weeks.

Actually, Judge Hinshaw did not get around to rendering judgment in the case until August 2, when he denied her a writ of mandamus that would order the University of Oklahoma to admit her. In delivering his opinion, he described the faculty of the Langston law school as "fully qualified." He held that the library of the new law school was equal in "all respects" to the library on the Norman campus and that the physical facility provided for the new school at the capitol building compared favorably with the "overcrowded conditions" at the university School of Law. In regard to class size the judge remarked that, in order to furnish "substantially equal" facilities, the state was not required to furnish a student body at the new law school of approximately the same size as the student body at the university law school. Mrs. Fisher's attorneys, no doubt disappointed by Judge Hinshaw's incredible conclusion that the Langston law school was equal to the university law school, indicated that their client would appeal.

3.

GEORGE W. McLAURIN

I have no evidence that any extensive preparations were made to appeal Mrs. Fisher's case. Instead, the attorneys for the NAACP apparently turned their major attention to the cases of the six Negroes who had been denied admission to the University of Oklahoma following their applications on January 28. Their efforts were centered largely around one of the six, George W. McLaurin, a fifty-four-year old applicant who on June 17 had petitioned the Cleveland County District Court for a writ of mandamus that would force the university to admit him to the Graduate College.[1] Similar petitions were filed on the same day for Helen Maxine Holmes and Mauderie Hancock. In filing their petitions, the plaintiffs used a slightly different list of defendants from the one that had been used in the Fisher case: the Board of Regents of the University of Oklahoma; President George L. Cross; Laurence Snyder, Dean of the Graduate College; and J. E. Fellows, Dean of Admissions. Judge Hinshaw received the filings, issued alternative writs of mandamus, and set hearings for July 19, 1948.

[1] G. W. McLaurin v. Board of Regents, University of Oklahoma, et al., "Petition for Writ of Mandamus," filed June 17, 1948.

In filing answer to the three petitions, the attorney general, again representing the University of Oklahoma, attacked the lateness of the applications for admission to the second semester. Inasmuch as the applications had been received the day before the semester began, the attorney general argued, it was "manifestly impossible" to provide the courses in question. He contended that the State Regents for Higher Education were entitled to a "reasonable time lapse" in providing the new course of instruction without violating the equal-protection clause.[2]

The reaction of the public to the renewal of legal activity was significant. For the first time since the litigation aimed at desegregation began, some Oklahomans appeared to become aware that there must finally be an end to segregation. Newspaper articles pointed out that, whereas Mrs. Fisher's suit had been successfully countered through the creation of the School of Law in the State Capitol Building, Oklahoma had no such recourse in the new cases that were developing.[3]

Public officials and educators throughout the state agreed in expressing doubt that the state would be able to set up an adequate graduate school at Langston that would offer all the fields of study that were available to white students. The committee of deans from the University of Oklahoma and Oklahoma A&M College had spotlighted this difficulty in its report to the state regents. Obviously, it would cost millions of dollars to duplicate the facilities of the University of Oklahoma, where

[2] *G. W. McLaurin* v. *Board of Regents, University of Oklahoma, et al.,* "Answer to Petition," filed July 16, 1948.
[3] *Daily Oklahoman,* June 18, 1948.

graduate work in seventy different fields was being offered to white students. It seemed clear that, as fast as a graduate program might be established in one field, application for another would be made.

For some reason, perhaps in an effort to expedite the desegregation process in Oklahoma, on July 26 McLaurin and his attorneys dropped the suit in the Cleveland County Court[4] and filed instead a complaint in the District Court of the United States for the Western District of Oklahoma. This complaint (Civil No. 4039)[5] stated that the jurisdiction of the District Court was

invoked under Judicial Code, Section 24 (1) (28 U.S.C., Section 41 (1)), this being a suit in equity which arises under the Constitution and laws of the United States, viz., the Fourteenth Amendment of said Constitution and Sections 41 and 42 of Title 8 of the United States Code, wherein the matter in controversy exceeds, exclusive of interest and costs, the sum of $3,000. The jurisdiction of this Court is also invoked under Judicial Code, Section 24 (14) (24 U.S.C., Section 41 (4)), this being a suit in equity authorized by law to be brought to redress the deprivation under color of law, statute, regulation, custom and usage of a state or rights, privileges and immunities secured by laws of the United States providing for equal rights of citizens of the United States and of all persons within the jurisdiction of the United States Code. The jurisdiction of this Court is also invoked under Judicial Code, Section 266 (28 U.S.C. Section 380), this being an action for an interlocutory injunction restraining the enforcement and execution of a state statute and restraining the order, policy, custom and

---

[4] *G. W. McLaurin* v. *Board of Regents, University of Oklahoma, et al.*, "Certificate of Dismissal Without Prejudice," July 26, 1948.

[5] Copy of "Complaint," August 5, 1948 (files of the Administration of the University of Oklahoma).

usage of an administrative board of a state pursuant to such statute.

The remainder of the complaint stated the case for the plaintiff much as it had been stated for Mrs. Fisher and asked that the court issue a permanent injunction restraining the defendants, their agents, and their employees from excluding the plaintiff and "others on whose behalf he sues" from admission to courses offered only at the Graduate College of the University of Oklahoma solely because of race or color. The complaint asked also that the plaintiff have judgment for five thousand dollars in damages.

On September 16, 1948, while awaiting action of the Federal District Court, McLaurin again applied for admission to the Graduate College of the University of Oklahoma, no doubt reasoning that he might be admitted because he had met the major objection made by the attorney general in the latter's reply to McLaurin's petition in the Cleveland County Court, namely, that he had not at the time of his previous application given the state sufficient notice that he desired to pursue a program in graduate education in Oklahoma. Once again he was denied admission because the state's laws concerning segregation were still in effect, and the results of previous court action involved only one Negro applicant, Mrs. Fisher.

Possibly taking into consideration the state's failure to provide a program for McLaurin at Langston, the Federal District Court, with Judges A. P. Murrah, Edgar S. Vaught, and Bower Broaddus presiding, accepted jurisdiction of the case and on September 29 ruled that

the plaintiff must be admitted to the University of Oklahoma or that the university must discontinue for white
students the course of study leading to a doctor's degree
in education—the program in which McLaurin sought to
enroll.[6] However, the ruling did not strike down the
state's segregation laws. In clarifying its opinion with
respect to this issue, the court stated: "This does not
mean, however, that the segregation laws of Oklahoma
are incapable of enforcement. We simply hold that in-
sofar as they are sought to be enforced in this particular
case they are inoperative." This clarifying statement,
together with the fact that the court did not issue an
injunction concerning the conditions under which
McLaurin should be admitted, provided opportunity for
more of the same kind of evasive action that had been so
prevalent in the Fisher case.

The university regents met on October 6 in special
session with Governor Turner and Attorney General
Williamson to consider this new development. The attorney general told the regents that they had a choice of
admitting McLaurin or discontinuing the program in
graduate education. He told the regents also that, if they
wished, they could create segregated classes at the university under the terms of the Federal District Court's
ruling. Williamson emphasized that the ruling did not
open wide the doors of white colleges in the state to
Negro students and that the ruling would apply only to
those who had previously applied for admission to the
University of Oklahoma for courses under conditions
similar to the McLaurin application. It would not apply

[6] 87 F. Supp. 526–28 (1948).

to students who might make application in the future.
It would not apply to Mrs. Fisher because the courts had
not yet decided whether Langston's new graduate law
school was equal to that of the University of Oklahoma.

Following their meeting with the governor and the
attorney general, the regents discussed the problem for
several hours. They finally decided that a study should
be made and a procedure developed for giving Negro
graduate students instruction "on a basis of complete
segregation." They postponed action on the admission
of McLaurin through the passage of a motion by Regent
T. R. Benedum of Norman, as follows:

I move that further consideration of the application of
G. W. McLaurin for admission to the graduate school of the
University be deferred until the next regular meeting of the
Board of Regents, and that President Cross be directed to
continue a study of a manner in which instructions on the
graduate level can be afforded to the applicant on a basis of
complete segregation.

That President Cross report to the board in detail at its
next regular meeting as to the hours that classrooms can be
made available and personnel of professors whose schedules
can be arranged so as to enable them to instruct applicant, all
to the end that he will be provided equal educational opportunities in the desired course in the Graduate School as those
afforded to any student in said school.

That President Cross further be instructed to contact the
Board of Regents for Higher Education or other appropriate
officers of the State of Oklahoma to procure additional funds
necessary to provide instructions to G. W. McLaurin on
a basis of complete segregation and report at the next meeting
of the board.[7]

[7] Board of Regents of the University of Oklahoma, "Minutes" October 6, 1948, 2879–80.

The action of the regents was reported to the press on Thursday, October 7, and Hall, McLaurin's attorney, immediately announced that he was sending a motion to the Federal District Court in Oklahoma City asking that an injunction be issued at once against university interference with McLaurin's application. In making the announcement, he admitted that it would be difficult to get a decision from the Federal District Court because Justice Murrah was to be away from Oklahoma City until November 18 or 20. During the next two days, however, the regents became uneasy about their decision to delay McLaurin's enrollment and the president of the board called another special meeting for Sunday, October 10.

It was never quite clear to me why the decision was made to call this special meeting. It may have been related to a rumor that McLaurin's attorneys had filed a petition with the United States Supreme Court asking the Court to force the university to admit McLaurin immediately. I learned later that Attorney General Williamson had received on Friday or Saturday a telegram from Justice Rutledge of the Supreme Court asking what the state was doing in the case. It could be that upon receipt of the telegram Williamson got in touch with the president of the university's board of regents. The realization that the case might come before the high court may have led to the decision to hold the special meeting and approve McLaurin's admission. In any event, following the meeting on Sunday, the regents released to the press the following statement:

Admission of G. W. McLaurin, Negro, to the University of

Oklahoma, on a segregated basis has been directed by the University of Oklahoma Board of Regents.

The action was taken at a special meeting Sunday when the board adopted the following resolution: "that the Board of Regents of the University of Oklahoma authorize and direct the President of the University and the appropriate officials of the University to grant the application for admission to the Graduate College of G. W. McLaurin in time for Mr. McLaurin to enroll at the beginning of the term, under such rules and regulations as to segregation as the President of the University shall consider to afford to Mr. G. W. McLaurin substantially equal educational opportunities as are afforded to other persons seeking the same education in the Graduate College, and that the President of the University promulgate such regulations."

After adopting the resolution, the board further declared that McLaurin be notified to report to the University Wednesday for matriculation.[8]

Notice of the regents' action was sent to McLaurin, and he was invited to appear at the university for enrollment on Wednesday, October 13. Unfortunately, I was scheduled to be in New York City on Monday, Tuesday, and Wednesday of that week, and the disagreeable details of working out McLaurin's attendance on a segregated basis were left to Vice Presidents Carl Mason Franklin and Roscoe Cate and Glenn Couch, Dean of the University College.

McLaurin decided to accept, at least tentatively, admission for instruction on a segregated basis. Apparently he was aided in his decision by his attorney and by Dunjee, who, he said, advised him to go through with his enrollment to "see how they're going to work this out."

[8] *Daily Oklahoman*, October 12, 1948.

McLaurin arrived at the university on Wednesday morning, October 13, with his wife, Hall, and Dunjee. They went to the graduate office, on the second floor of the Administration Building. Joseph C. Pray, Associate Dean of the Graduate School, visited with McLaurin and then sent him on to see John F. Bender, the adviser for graduate students interested in educational administration, who helped him work out his schedule of classes. He completed his enrollment that afternoon. He was the first of his race to be admitted to the University of Oklahoma. He was quoted in the evening papers of that day as saying that he was "pleased with the reception that he had received at the University." He went on to elaborate: "Everything seemed to be natural and usual, and I really enjoyed being here today. Everything seemed to work out all right. I am pleased with the way the officials have received me and by their attitude in giving me information."[9]

I returned home the afternoon of the day McLaurin enrolled, and in a conference with Roscoe Cate and other members of my staff it was decided that, rather than set up special classes for McLaurin, we should devise some plan whereby he could attend classes with white students, but be sufficiently "segregated" to avoid penalty under the state laws.

McLaurin had enrolled in four courses in the College of Education, at that time housed in the old Carnegie Building, just off the northeast corner of the Administration Building. On the south side of the first floor of this building was Room 104, which consisted of a main sec-

[9] *Oklahoma City Times*, October 13, 1948.

tion and a little anteroom on its north side. The anteroom was separated, in a sense, from the rest of the room by columns, through which an occupant could have a clear view of the blackboard on the west side of the room, though at an angle of about forty-five degrees. With some misgivings whether the arrangement would meet the test of the state segregation laws, it was decided that all McLaurin's classes would be held in this room, that he would have his seat in the anteroom, and that the anteroom would not be considered a part of the classroom—it would be considered a separate, though adjoining, area.

McLaurin went to his first class at 2:00 P.M. on Thursday, October 14. He arrived about ten minutes early and quietly seated himself at a desk which had been placed in the alcove. The course was one in educational psychology, taught by Professor F. A. Balyeat. The class had been scheduled for a room upstairs in the building, but when the students assembled there, Professor Balyeat explained the situation and said that he had been instructed to take the class to Room 104 where McLaurin was waiting.

McLaurin's first class session at the university was, of course, an occasion of great curiosity for students, reporters, and photographers. It was also an occasion of considerable tension for the administration and for Professor Balyeat. While waiting for class to start, a number of curious students, teachers, and others looked into the room but said nothing to McLaurin. Finally, according to an article in the *Daily Oklahoman* of October 15, two students approached McLaurin and told him that they

wanted to welcome him to the university. They expressed the hope that he would "find a warm welcome"
from others. The two students introduced themselves as
George Bassett and Edith Long. McLaurin acknowl-
edged their introductions with a smile and commented,
"How do you do? I guess you know that my name is
McLaurin."

Separate toilet facilities for McLaurin were provided
on the first floor of the Education Building. It was arranged that he would eat alone in the Student Union's
short-order room, known as "the Jug," between 12:00
and 1:00 P.M. daily; there was no provision for breakfast
or dinner. A separate table, marked with his name, was
provided in the stacks just off the main reading room in
the university library.

On the whole, McLaurin seemed satisfied with the
arrangements that had been made for him, though, when
questioned after his first class whether he thought that
he would receive equal educational opportunity in the
situation, he replied that it was hard to tell. He commented that the presence of photographers in the classroom and the noise of repair work down the hall had
made it difficult for him to concentrate.

Newspaper reporters and photographers covered the
events of McLaurin's first day so thoroughly that for the
next few days I was concerned that some citizen might
go to court in an effort to force the university to observe
Oklahoma's segregation laws more closely. My concern
was based on the fact that I did not have a very precise
understanding of my position in relation to the state laws
or to the opinion that had been handed down by the

Federal District Court on September 29 and the interpretation of this opinion, which had been given by Attorney General Williamson. While the Federal District
Court found "null and void" those sections of the Oklahoma segregation laws that denied McLaurin equal
educational opportunities at a state-supported school, the
court did not order McLaurin admitted to the University
of Oklahoma on a nonsegregated basis. The attorney
general had interpreted the court's ruling as permitting
the regents of the university to approve his enrollment
on a basis of segregation, and the regents had ordered
me to enroll him "under such rules and regulations as to
segregation" as would afford him the same education in
the Graduate College as is afforded to other students.
Despite the attorney general's ruling and the regents'
instructions, I was not sure what protection the Federal
District Court's ruling gave me in experimenting with
the state's segregation laws, but fortunately no one decided to challenge the university's procedures in court.

It was obvious, however, that further litigation on
behalf of the plaintiff was in the offing when Thurgood
Marshall came to Oklahoma from New York City on
Friday, October 15. Marshall announced that the purpose of his visit was to consult with attorneys of the local
branch of the NAACP concerning additional efforts to
attack Oklahoma's segregation laws. He was caustically
critical of the plan that had been worked out for
McLaurin and described it, perhaps aptly, as "stupid"
when questioned by photographers at the Oklahoma
City airport.

Following the special meeting of the university re-

Six Negro students applied for admission to the University of Oklahoma on January 29, 1948. Seated, left to right: Ivor Tatum, Oklahoma City; Mosell A. Dillon, Langston; Helen Holmes, Oklahoma City; Mauderie Hancock Wilson, Oklahoma City; James Bond, Langston; George W. McLaurin, Oklahoma City. Standing: President Cross (left) and Dean of Admissions Fellows. Courtesy University of Oklahoma Archives.

Miss Ruth Arnold, director of admissions at the University of Oklahoma, receives an application for admission from George W. McLaurin, the first Negro to be admitted to the university, October, 1948. Courtesy *Oklahoman and Times.*

Dean Fellows approves the admission of McLaurin and discusses enrollment procedures with him. Courtesy *Oklahoman and Times.*

McLaurin being welcomed to the University of Oklahoma by George
Bassett, Norman, and Edith Long, Roanoke, Virginia, October, 1948.
Courtesy *Oklahoman and Times*.

McLaurin attends his first class at the University under segregated conditions. The lecturer is Professor F. A. Balyeat, of the College of Education. Courtesy *Oklahoman and Times*.

McLaurin with his wife, Peninah S. McLaurin. Mrs. McLaurin was the first Negro to apply for admission to the University of Oklahoma, in 1923. She was refused. Courtesy *Oklahoman and Times.*

Mrs. Fisher, shown when she returned to the University of Oklahoma in the fall of 1962 to begin work for a master's degree in history. Courtesy *Oklahoman and Times.*

Mrs. Fisher, shown when she returned to the University of Oklahoma campus on July 13, 1974, for a visit with President Emeritus Cross.

gents on October 7, when the board decided to delay
McLaurin's admission until their meeting in November,
McLaurin, through his attorney, had filed a petition with
the Federal District Court on October 8. The petition
asked for an order that would force the university to
admit him on a nonsegregated basis. The Federal District
Court had retained jurisdiction in the case and had
announced that a hearing on the petition would be held
on October 25.

The hearing was held as scheduled, and the morning
was spent largely in receiving evidence from McLaurin
concerning his segregated status at the University of
Oklahoma, supplemented by the repeated insistence of
Marshall that the court should modify its order of September
29 to place McLaurin in the university on a
completely desegregated basis. At noon the court dismissed
all witnesses, and Judge Murrah announced that
the case would be decided on briefs presented by the
opposing attorneys.

The decision of the three federal judges was not forthcoming
until Monday, November 22, 1948. On that day
the judges denied McLaurin's petition, stating in part,
"It is the duty of this Court to honor the public policy of
the state in matters relating to its internal social affairs
quite as much as it is our duty to vindicate the supreme
law of the land." The ruling stated also that "the Constitution
does not authorize us to obliterate social or racial
distinctions which the state has traditionally recognized
as a basis for classification for purposes of education and
other public ministrations."

"Further," continued the ruling, "the Fourteenth

Amendment does not abolish distinctions based upon race or color, nor was it intended to enforce social equality between classes and races. . . . segregation based upon racial distinctions is in accord with the deeply rooted social policy of the State of Oklahoma."

Taking note of McLaurin's testimony that he had been treated as an inferior and that he had been unable to concentrate because he had to sit at a designated desk separated from those of white students in his classes, was required to take his library books to a certain desk and study there alone, and was admitted to the school cafeteria only at specified times and had to eat at a table by himself, the judges stated:

> The plaintiff is now being afforded the same educational facilities as other students at the University of Oklahoma. . . . we cannot find any justifiable legal basis for the mental discomfiture which plaintiff says deprives him of equal educational opportunities here.
>
> We conclude, therefore, that the classification based on racial distinctions as recognized and enforced by the regulations of the University of Oklahoma, rests upon a reasonable foundation, having its foundation in the public policy of the State.

After receiving news of the ruling, Negro leaders announced that an appeal would be made to the United States Supreme Court. The appeal was made, and the high court began its study of the case in March, 1949. An opinion was not be forthcoming, however, until June 5, 1950.

With one Negro enrolled in the university and attending classes regularly, there was considerable speculation on the campus about what the next developments would be. It was anticipated that additional applications would be received for admission to the second semester of the 1948–49 academic year. Late in January, 1949, three such applications were received: one from Julius Caesar Hill, of Tulsa, who wanted to do work in graduate engineering; one from Mauderie Hancock Wilson, of Oklahoma City, who sought graduate work in sociology; and one from Mrs. Mary Weaver, also of Oklahoma City.

Mauderie Wilson had applied previously, and after refusal had unsuccessfully sought redress in the District Court of Cleveland County. She had then appealed her case to the state supreme court. During the McLaurin hearing before the Federal District Court in Oklahoma City, the NAACP attorneys had sought to have her included with McLaurin for action by that court. The court had refused because her case was still pending before the state supreme court.

Each of the three Negroes who applied late in January was academically qualified to enter the university, but the legal position of the university in relation to the state laws, court decisions, and so on, was not clear, and the university regents had instructed me to ask the attorney general for an opinion each time a Negro applied for enrollment. Accordingly, I asked Attorney General Williamson for an opinion concerning each of the three applicants. He ruled in effect that a Negro was eligible to enter the university if the program he sought was not offered by a Negro college in the state and if his application had been pending long enough to demonstrate that the state had failed to take steps to provide the program in a Negro college. By the time I received his opinion, applications for admission had arrived from two more Negroes: Mrs. Orpherita Daniels, of Oklahoma City, who wanted to study social work; and Mrs. Mary Motley, who wished to enroll in pharmacy, an undergraduate program. Under the attorney general's ruling it was possible to admit four of these applicants, but not Mauderie Wilson, who, according to the attorney general's ruling, did not give the state sufficient notice that she sought a program at the graduate level in sociology.

The complexity and absurdity of the situation was by this time becoming manifest. The State Regents for Higher Education, following a meeting on January 29, publicly announced a request that the state laws be changed to permit enrollment of Negroes in graduate or specialized Oklahoma schools for whites. Included in this request was the board's statement that it would be "both wise and expedient" to admit qualified Negro students to white colleges and universities if they could not get desired courses at Langston University.

In response to this request, Senator James A. Rinehart of El Reno expressed the opinion that it would not be necessary for the legislature to amend the state segregation laws because the three-judge Federal District Court in Oklahoma City had "taken care of that." But the *Norman Transcript* spotlighted the problem effectively in an editorial on February 7, 1949:

> The latest opinion of the state attorney general on attempts of several Negroes to enrol in the University shows that the issue is now so deeply involved in technicalities that action by the Legislature to clear up the situation is sorely needed.

The attorney general holds that a Negro is eligible to enter the University only if the course he wants to take is not offered by a Negro college and his application has been pending long enough to make certain that the state has failed to take steps to provide that course in a Negro college.

Thus he holds that a Negro who has waited a year to take graduate courses in social sciences is now eligible to enter the University, but it is up to the regents to decide whether a Negro who has waited only three and one-half months to take similar courses has waited long enough for the state to provide them in a Negro college.

All of that is nonsense. The Legislature should enact at this session legislation opening white colleges to Negroes for such work as the Langston college does not offer and is not likely to offer in the near future. This is in line with the recommendation of the Oklahoma regents for higher education.

After giving careful thought to the dilemma, I decided that only Mrs. Daniels could be admitted under the rulings of the attorney general; the remaining applications must await the February 9 meeting of the university regents. At that meeting, the regents approved the applications of Mrs. Daniels and Mrs. Wilson but denied admission to Julius Caesar Hill and Mrs. Motley because, in accordance with the attorney general's ruling, their applications had been received too late to allow the state a reasonable amount of time to set up separate schools. The regents instructed me to establish segregated facilities for Mrs. Daniels and Mrs. Wilson as had been provided for McLaurin.

During the following weeks the realization gradually developed in the minds of Oklahomans that the state would need to adjust to the idea of having Negroes in previously all-white colleges and universities. Attorney

General Williamson, perhaps somewhat influenced by the endless effort required to prepare opinions concerning applications presented by Negroes at the university, aligned himself with the regents in attempting to persuade the legislature to enact legislation admitting Negroes to colleges and universities in the state when the programs they desired were not available to them in a Negro college or university. As early as April, 1949, he urged the legislature to take positive action.[10] He warned that a continuation of the hands-off policy would ultimately result in a court order opening the graduate colleges to any Negro not finding courses available at Langston. Referring to the university's practice of referring to him all applications for admission by Negroes, he told reporters that for over a year he had served as registrar for the University of Oklahoma—a service made necessary, he said, because the segregation statutes were still in effect in Oklahoma, except as they had been specifically struck down in the McLaurin case. He urged the legislature to amend or repeal the segregation laws, either on a basis whereby Negroes would be allowed to attend white colleges under conditions of segregation, as determined by the governing boards of each institution, or that the segregation statutes be suspended in those cases where courses offered at white colleges were not offered at Langston.[11]

Despite the request of the state regents, the urging of the attorney general, and the obvious hopelessness of

[10] John Thomas Hubbell, "Racial Desegregation at the University of Oklahoma, 1946–1950" (M.A. thesis, University of Oklahoma, 1961), 52.
[11] *Ibid.*, 53.

preserving segregation at the graduate level, sentiment in the Oklahoma legislature favorable to amending the segregation laws did not develop until very late in the session. Finally a bill was introduced by Representative Edgar Boatman of Okmulgee providing that Negroes might be admitted for graduate work in any of the state's institutions of higher learning if the courses desired were not offered at Langston University. However, Boatman's bill did not repeal or amend the state's segregation laws; it merely provided that they were to be suspended in part under the conditions described—specifically, that Negroes should be admitted on a segregated basis but that the governing boards of the various colleges should determine what was meant by a "segregated basis."

While I was disappointed that the bill provided for admission on a segregated basis, I did feel that some progress had been made through the provision that the governing boards should determine what segregation meant.

I was scheduled to leave for a trip to Chicago before the bill was passed, but I went to the airport with a feeling of satisfaction that we might be approaching a solution to this long-standing, vexing problem. I did not learn until my return to Norman that on the last day of the legislative session the senate, influenced by Senator Bill Logan of Lawton, President Pro Tempore, had managed to get the bill amended to read "segregated basis is defined in this act as classroom instruction given in separate classrooms or at separate times."

Officials of the colleges and universities of Oklahoma who had been concerned with the segregation features of the bill before it was amended were appalled by the prospective costs of providing separate classrooms and teachers for Negro students. John B. Cheadle, Professor of Law and legal adviser to the regents, responded to the university's request for an interpretation of the new law by writing to Vice-President Carl Mason Franklin:

I assume that the intent of this act is to have Negroes separated from Whites following a pattern to be gleaned from the various statutes. I assume that it will be construed to mean separate class facilities, separate living quarters, separate eating provisions (Negroes may not be eaten by lions or tigers which heretofore have eaten only white people), and separate rest rooms, etc. This 1949 act will cause us a great deal of trouble.

Cheadle's pessimistic prophecy was to be fully realized during the weeks ahead.

However, the attorney general provided a most helpful ruling concerning the new law: he announced that the decision about what constitutes a separate classroom would be left to university officials. Officials at the university promptly decided that a roped-off or railed-off section of a room would constitute an additional room, thus providing two separate rooms where only one had existed before. Plans were launched immediately to provide programs for the eleven Negroes who had enrolled at the university for the summer session, all of whom were to do work at the graduate level. One Negro veteran of World War II, Malcomb Smith Whitby, of Oklahoma City, was among the eleven who had enrolled. Plans also were formulated for the twenty-three additional applicants who had applied for enrollment but had not been admitted because the state regents had not informed the university whether the courses they sought were offered at Langston. Of the twenty-three with pending applications, several were undergraduates.

With the passage of the new law the state regents decided to close the Langston law school, effective on June 30, 1949. When Mrs. Fisher read this announcement, she understandably assumed that she now would be permitted to enroll in the School of Law at the university. But when she came to the institution for that purpose on June 17, the admissions office denied her application on the technical grounds that a legal education was still available to her at the branch of Langston University in Oklahoma City and that under the provisions of the new state segregation statute her admission to the university could not be approved. Word of the denial came to my office that afternoon, and, after reflecting for a few minutes on the possible consequences of violating the state's most recent statute on segregation, I decided it would be absurd not to permit the young woman to get under way immediately with her legal education. If she were required to wait until the Law School for Negroes in Oklahoma City had passed out of existence on June 30, it would be too late for her to enroll in the summer session at the university. It seemed impractical to require her to attend the school in Oklahoma City until June 30 and then transfer to the university's School of Law. Accordingly, I sent instructions to the admissions office that she should be admitted immediately. This was accomplished the following day, June 18, when she enrolled as a first-year law student on the

Norman campus, more than three years after her first application.

Twelve days later, on June 30, the Langston Law School was closed and discontinued. During its short existence it attracted only one enrollee, T. M. Roberts, of Oklahoma City. Roberts enrolled at the beginning of the final semester of the school's existence. When the school was discontinued, the credits he had earned were transferred to the University of Oklahoma, where he resumed his program the following autumn. However, I believe that he remained at the university for only one semester.

4.

REACTIONS

The decision to use rails and ropes to establish separate classrooms for Negroes was bitterly assailed by Senate President Pro Tem Logan. He wrote to me on June 18:

> There is nothing ambiguous about the statute. The legislature made it clear that it wanted to provide equal educational facilities for Negroes, and at the same time maintain Oklahoma's respected and traditional segregation laws.
>
> According to newspaper reports, the University is considering the placing of railings or ropes or some other such imaginary division lines in classrooms. My personal opinion is that such a separation is an insult to the colored students and violates the spirit of the Constitution of the United States because of lack of dignity for the individual. The University, if it wants to follow such a subterfuge, would be more honest if it merely seated the students in a room together without such division lines. Such a seating arrangement, in my opinion, will be photographed and printed in national newspapers and magazines for the purpose of bringing scorn and disrespect for Oklahoma. I know that such a procedure encourages scorn and disrespect for the act passed by the legislature.

Logan spoke freely to reporters concerning his displeasure with the university's action. He was quoted in several papers as saying:

The railing itself is an insult to the law, to the legislature and to the colored people. The University of Oklahoma is disregarding the plain wording of the law. I think they are trying to bring down condemnation of the law. If the University wants to disregard the law, it should take down the railings and admit that it is disregarding the law.

However, Representative Boatman, author of the statute in the house and at the time a student of law at the university, suggested that Logan was engaging in "petty politics" designed to "boost himself into the 1950 gubernatorial race on a platform of white supremacy."[1] Many on the Norman campus agreed with Boatman's appraisal.

I decided to ignore the senator's protest, and we finally started the summer session with a total of twenty-three Negro students enrolled in forty classes. All of the entrants, with the exception of Mrs. Fisher, used "segregated" classrooms consisting of roped- or railed-off portions of main rooms. The structure of the law classrooms did not lend themselves to such marking, and a sign "For Colored" was used to indicate segregated seating. Outside the classrooms, segregation was complete— separate eating facilities, reading areas in the library, rest rooms, and so on. Because I suspected that Senator Logan, and perhaps others, might have protested to the regents of the university, I prepared a careful and, I hoped, persuasive report, which I presented to the board at a meeting on June 29. I was pleased—and slightly surprised—when our interpretation of "separate class-

[1] *Daily Oklahoman*, June 9, 1949.

rooms" was unanimously approved after only a short discussion.[2]

The segregation plan worked comparatively well, except that the white students showed an occasional inclination to remove the barricades and on two or three occasions cut up the ropes separating the classrooms for souvenirs. The law students in Mrs. Fisher's class promptly carried off the "For Colored" sign. Other white students (or perhaps the same ones) frequently violated the state's segregation laws by eating their meals at the same tables with the Negro students or by studying with them in the library.

Senator Logan's protest was the last that I received from any individual of political importance in the state, but my office continued to receive a great deal of pressure from various groups and individuals who opposed desegregation or, conversely, who thought that it was not being accomplished rapidly enough. An activist student group, the Equal Education Committee, conducted a number of informal polls on the campus and used the results in preparing a petition that they delivered to my office. The petition requested that all signs having to do with segregation be removed from the campus on the grounds that they constituted an "outrageous display of racism" that was humiliating and disgusting to most white students, as well as to Negroes. The petition alleged that a large majority of the student body opposed segregation in any form.

While I was in agreement with most of the points

[2] Board of Regents of the University of Oklahoma, "Minutes," June 29, 1949, 3179.

contained in the petition, I could only point out to the committee that my hands were tied by state laws and emphasize the need to handle the situation judiciously so that what progress had been made in desegregation would not be negated. I wrote to the committee: "Although I appreciate having your expression of opinion, I believe that it would be best that I not be influenced in any way by any group, that I use my own best judgment as to how these problems can be worked out at the University of Oklahoma."

As might be expected, the national publicity following nearly every action taken on the campus resulted in many phone calls and a number of letters presenting both sides of the question.[3] One indignant Californian wrote that "[it is] ever so clear to me now why your breed of American is called the 'Oakie-type,' and called that with a mixture of genuine pity and contempt." A second writer was specific in his description of university officials when he declared: "You are the most contemptible yellow dogs under a tolerant God's sun. I hope the government throws all of you in jail." From a third came the suggestion that Oklahoma segregation policies made a "mockery of all our colleges are supposed to teach." A fourth charged that the university was "really trying to make the state of Oklahoma look ridiculous, for you

[3] This correspondence was explored carefully by John Thomas Hubbell, who used racial desegregation at the University of Oklahoma as the topic for an excellent master's thesis in the Department of History (1961). Hubbell selected excerpts from the various letters, which he included in his account. The examples given here were taken from those quoted by Hubbell.

would take even such as Al Capone, were he living, but would reject George Washington Carver, or Marian Anderson, only because of an insignificant difference. Silly, isn't it, when one thinks a minute?" A resident of Seattle suggested that, "since education and progress go hand in hand, education in your college hasn't progressed since the founding of the college."

A woman in New Jersey expressed the opinion that McLaurin was "probably far superior to those of you who in your stupid, arrogant, superiority plan to segregate him." Another New Jersey woman wondered, "How narrow and hard can an educated person or school be not to wish to share its advantages with another human being, regardless of color?" A student at Vassar suggested the possibility of "a little Jim Crow place in heaven."

Letters of similar tone were received from throughout the country, and came in substantial numbers from the Middle West. An alumna of the University of Oklahoma offered this thought "It is incidents such as the Sipuel case which furnish fuel for disparaging comments by the Russian press. The Russians seize upon anything which is undemocratic or discriminatory for publication and vilify our way of life." The international implications of the situation were pointed up also by a member of the League of Women Voters in the state of Washington, who asked, "How can we tell the world Hitler was wrong in his race superiority when the highest institutions of education at home force this program upon its people?" But a resident of the state of Texas interpreted the international implications differently. She suspected that a

Communist plot was involved in the effort to break the segregation laws. In her letter she urged the South to

fight all the Communist or Socialist inspired negro demands for entrance to white universities, not because the negro is interested in the subjects . . . but because he is the tool of the Communist-Socialist supported organization the National Association for the Advancement of Colored People.

It remained for an Oklahoman to inject religion into the controversy. In his letter he stated that

Jesus Christ did not preach social equality. The Negro . . . was created a black race . . . Nature gave him flesh and glands that throws off a stink to protect him against moskitoes and insects so that he could inhabit low swampy lands. . . . Nothing pleases the negro more than to mix his blood with the whites. With white man's blood in him he is wiser and meaner. . . . The mixed breeds cause all the trouble. Anti segregation laws mean the negro bucks are free to marry our Daughters.

Marital mixing of the races stemming from the abolition of segregation laws obviously was a major source of concern to many Oklahomans. They expressed their fears in several letters to my office and probably in many similar communications to members of the state legislature. But insecurity of another kind was frequently expressed:

We have had plenty of trouble in that school. Remember when everlution broke out. We had a Bankers son told us about it and he fell for it. I said your folks may be monkys but Im not and neither are my people. I got the Bible, in the first book in the Bible, where God made man, and blew breath into his nostrils, never said a word about a monky, that settled his part. Now here we are faced with the negro. I dont suppose you lived in Okla. when we Jim Crowed the negros. They voted, and would push our men around and tried on my husband but he was a Texan and so am I. He lifted him out by the collar, after that they all liked him and called him a real white man, tipped their hats to me.

When Dewey was running for president, the negroes would gather on the corners of the white town, laugh and carry on. Several old Negro women who had worked for our good Christian women, would charge $5.00 per day for company. One day a good member of my church met this old Auntie on the street and asked her if she knew anyone she could get to help her till she was well. She said no mam's Ise looking for some help myself. She said just wait till President Dewey gets in office, we'll have a white woman in ever niggers kitchen. As Dewey wasn't President well they went back to negro town and quit laughing.

If I wanted my Grandchildren and children to go to a negro school, I would live where they could. Kansas University is one, there are lots. Here is my prayer, you may not be there to finish, but some of the rest may. We pay taxes to support our state school and lets keep it from some people who is trying to break it up. You know Dewey is running again Lord help us.

Hubbell suggested, appropriately enough, that letters and other communications of this sort were in part responsible for the legislature's reluctance to take proper action on the segregation issue.

Despite the continuing struggle in the courts, many Negroes seemed satisfied with the university's efforts to cope with the situation. One prominent Negro resident of Oklahoma wrote that

... in the main Negro students were receiving good treatment and that their instructors and the student body had been unusually fine in their attitude toward them. Everyone seemingly feels that the University's authorities are doing all that they possibly can within the precincts of the recent law passed by the legislature.

Another, who had attended the commencement ceremonies of 1950, wrote to thank the "white people who has made it possible for the qualified colored people to enter your grand School of Education. . . . I hope they will make good with the great opportunity." An understanding Negro army sergeant suggested that, although the university could not "abolish the racial differences throughout our America, you can at least continue to grind it down in your locality and by doing others will see your good works and will be constrained to follow you."

Unfortunately for the university, only a relatively few people appeared to have an understanding of the complicated legal aspects of the struggle. Blame was seldom placed where it belonged—on the Oklahoma legislature for not rescinding the offending state laws and the Supreme Court of the United States for not declaring those laws unconstitutional.

During the summer of 1949 segregation outside the classroom was maintained in reasonable compliance with the state laws. A special study area in the university library was provided with tables marked "Reserved for Negroes," a snack bar in the Student Union Building was reserved for Negro students during the noon hour, with separate tables labeled in the dining hall for service at other times, and separate rest rooms in several buildings were marked for the use of Negroes.

But a new facet of the problem emerged in September, 1949, when a male Negro applied for university housing. In response to his application the regents directed me to explore the possibility—in terms of cost, locations, and sources of funds—of providing separate housing for at least fifty Negro men and fifty Negro women. After going into the matter with the university architect, I was forced to report to the board at its October meeting that the projects were not feasible. The cost would be approximately $150,000 for each building, and only one Negro man and one Negro woman had asked for university housing. I recommended, and the regents approved, that Negroes be housed in the "prefabs" that had been constructed south of the campus following the close of World War II.

Another difficulty soon developed concerning the use of the Student Union Building by Negroes who were not enrolled in the university but had come to the campus to attend conferences or short courses. The first instance of this particular problem occurred early in 1947 when three members of the faculty at Langston University, who were attending a conference on audio-visual classroom aids, were refused food service. The problem was complicated by the fact that the Oklahoma Memorial Union was (and is) a separate corporation owned and controlled by a board of governors operating in a facility constructed on land leased from the university. Hence the extent to which laws concerning segregation at institutions of higher learning in Oklahoma applied to activities within the building was somewhat obscure. But following the incident involving the three faculty members from Langston, the university administration conceded that the union could refuse service to non-student members of the Negro race if the management decided to do so.

Early in 1948 a member of the faculty took a Negro guest with him to the union building and received service in the cafeteria. Although the incident apparently was practically unnoticed by other customers that day, the management of the union was understandably concerned about what might develop in the future and asked the president's office for a statement of policy. Professor Cheadle, called in for another interpretation of state law, suggested that if Negroes were merely visiting the university, including the Student Union Building, and were not there as students but as "invitees for some other purpose," the segregation laws need not apply. It was agreed that this policy would be followed quietly—without any announcement that might excite the state's segregationists. This procedure worked out rather well, and during the next few weeks visiting Negroes occasionally used the facilities of the Union Building without causing comment of any kind.

But later in 1948 the problem was again spotlighted when a representative of the student senate requested a ruling whether the lounge in the Union Building might be used for a mixed reception of white and Negro students during a conference on student government. It was expected that Negroes would attend the conference, and the local students wanted the way cleared for them to attend any events scheduled in the Union Building.

Ted Beaird, manager of the union, decided that this type of activity probably was not covered by the policy that had been quietly adopted earlier for Negro visitors to the campus, and so he posed the question to his board of governors by mail. The board voted four to three against permitting mixed receptions in the building. Beaird then ruled that facilities of the Oklahoma Memorial Union could not be booked for "assembly of white and colored students, under present regulations."

With the increased enrollment of Negroes during the summer of 1949—and the prospect of an additional increase in the fall—it was necessary to give attention to the problem of seating Negroes at athletic contests sponsored by the university. Football at the institution had emerged into national prominence, and it was assumed that Negroes in the student body, and perhaps other Negroes as well, would want to see the games. The regents took a close look at this problem at their meeting in July and decided that the state's segregation law applied in the stadium as well as in the classroom. However, it was decided also that the same interpretation of what constituted segregated facilities should apply in the stadium as had been used in the classroom. If a portion of a classroom separated from the remainder by a barrier, such as a rope or a railing, meant that the separated portion was a separate room, then a portion of the stadium separated from the remainder by a similar barrier could be regarded as providing segregated facilities.

Accordingly, a plywood barrier was erected in the northeastern portion of the stadium, which separated a small section reserved for Negroes. Both Negroes and whites accepted this solution, and the only complaint I received came from Negroes who reported that the white students sitting in front of it used the barrier as a back rest and pushed it into their laps.

There were various suggestions as to what might be done; perhaps a rope or chain should be used instead of the plywood. Vice-President Franklin thought that we could "get by" if the barrier was removed and the seats were marked "Reserved for Negroes." After discussing this possibility informally with the members of the governing board, it was decided not to experiment with the state laws in such a highly visible manner; the plywood barrier was braced and left for the remainder of the season.

Happily, the university had to endure this ridiculous and extremely embarrassing situation for only one academic year. McLaurin's appeal came before the United States Supreme Court the following spring, 1950. At the hearing Fred Hansen, the assistant attorney general for the state of Oklahoma, appeared to base his argument on the premise that racial problems were gradually being solved but that the segregation statutes needed to be retained on at least a temporary basis in order to bring about an orderly solution. He predicted that a chaotic situation would develop should these statutes be invalidated by action of the Supreme Court. When questioned, he admitted that whites and Negroes currently enrolled at the university seemed to be getting along without

friction, but he attributed this to the fact that only graduate students were involved at the moment. He thought
that difficulties might develop if there should be mixed
enrollments of undergraduates.

The NAACP attorneys centered their argument on the
basic injustice of racial segregation. They took the position that neither race nor ancestry was pertinent to the
objectives of public education. They alleged that segregation tended to encourage and increase distrust and
spotlight differences between Negroes and other races
that were not pertinent in educational processes.

Justice Jackson effectively summed up the arguments
of the plaintiff's attorneys by inquiring whether it would
be a fair statement to say that "there can be no separate
treatment of Negro and white students that is equal.
Under this cultural question you seek to raise, isn't it
your complaint that a Negro is identified as a Negro?"
To this, Robert L. Carter, an NAACP attorney, replied,
"Yes, sir, that is exactly our position." He went on to state
that the University had no right to enforce rules applying
to Negroes that did not apply also to whites.[4]

On June 5, 1950, the Supreme Court ruled unanimously in favor of McLaurin. It responded to his claim
that the restrictions of segregation imposed upon him at
the University of Oklahoma did "impair and inhibit his
ability to study, to engage in discussion, and exchange
views with other students, and in general to learn his
profession" by stating in the second paragraph of the
syllabus prepared by Chief Justice Fred M. Vinson that

[4] *Ibid.*, 65.

the equal protection clause of the Fourteenth Amendment is violated when a state, after admitting a Negro student to graduate instruction in its state university, affords him, solely because of his race, different treatment from other students, as by requiring him to occupy a seat in a row in the classroom specified for colored students, or at a designated table in the library, or at a special table in the cafeteria.

The ruling provided that "state imposed restrictions which produced such inequality cannot be sustained." Thus the Court reversed the decision of the three-judge Federal District Court for the Western District of Oklahoma, and accomplished for the Negro race what should have been accomplished more than four years earlier.[5]

The long-awaited decision was hailed with enthusiasm by officials of the University of Oklahoma, its faculty, most students, and a substantial portion of the state's citizenry. The NAACP attorneys regarded it as a "complete victory." The enthusiasm was increased by the realization that the decision did not apply solely to the University of Oklahoma; it meant that Negroes now would be admitted to graduate study in all state-supported colleges and universities in the country. Desegregation had been accomplished for the nation in a portion of higher education—but only in a portion.

[5] *McLaurin* v. *Oklahoma State Regents for Higher Education et al.*, 339 U.S. 637, 94 L.Ed. 1149 (1950).

5.

EPILOGUE

Many readers will recall with regret that four more
years were to elapse before desegregation was accomplished in the public schools—elementary and secondary
—of the country. It was not until May 17, 1954 that the
Supreme Court of the United States, after hearing the
case of *Brown* v. *Board of Education of Topeka, Kansas,*
and four consolidated cases from South Carolina, Virginia, the District of Columbia, and Delaware, unanimously reversed its former doctrine of "separate but
equal" and held, in a decision prepared by Chief Justice
Warren, that

it is doubtful that any child may reasonably be expected to
succeed in life if he is denied the opportunity of an education.
Such an opportunity, where the state has undertaken to provide it, is a right which must be made available to all on equal
terms. We come then to the question presented: Does segregation of children in public schools solely on the basis of race,
even though the physical facilities and other "tangible" factors
may be equal, deprive the children of the minority group of
equal educational opportunities? We believe that it does.
Whatever may have been the extent of psychological knowledge at the time of Plessy v. Ferguson, this finding is amply

supported by modern authority. Any language in Plessy v. Ferguson contrary to this finding is rejected.

We conclude that in the field of public education the doctrine of "separate but equal" has no place. Separate educational facilities are inherently unequal. Therefore, we hold that the plaintiffs and others similarly situated for whom the actions have been brought are, by reason of the segregation complained of, deprived of the equal protection of the laws guaranteed by the Fourteenth Amendment.

. . . In order that we may have the full assistance of the parties in formulating decrees, the cases will be restored to the docket, and the parties are requested to present further argument on Questions 4 and 5 previously propounded by the Court for the reargument this term. The Attorney General of the United States is again invited to participate. The Attorneys General of the states requiring or permitting segregation in public education will also be permitted to appear as amici curiae upon request to do so by September 15, 1954, and submission of briefs by October 1, 1954.

It is so ordered.[1]

While this pronouncement apparently expressed the beliefs and attitudes of the members of the Supreme Court concerning "separate but equal" educational opportunities, it contained no instructions upon which those responsible for the nation's schools could base action. It did not nullify the segregation laws of the states involved, and it did not order the admission of Negroes to the schools. It merely held that the plaintiffs involved in the case had been deprived of the equal protection of the laws guaranteed by the Fourteenth Amendment. It was not a final decree but merely an announcement that further action would be forthcoming. It was an invitation

---

[1] 347 U.S. 483, 98 L.Ed. 873 (1954).

to the states involved to appear, upon "request to do so," and present certain additional arguments before a final decree would be announced. It left unanswered certain questions concerning desegregation in undergraduate higher education.

The Oklahoma State Regents for Higher Education explored the pronouncement of the Supreme Court carefully at their regular meeting on October 25, 1954, and issued the following statement of policy for the guidance of the constituent institutions of the Oklahoma system:

The Regents are obliged to work within the provisions of the existing Oklahoma laws. Until final decrees otherwise are handed down by a court of competent jurisdiction, and until such decrees are legally implemented, or until the legislature changes the Oklahoma laws, we expect to observe the yet existing statutes.

It appears to us that the applicable statutes are as stated on page 861, Title 70, Sections 455, 456, 457, O.S. 1951.

The Langston offerings will accomodate practically all undergraduates. Some Negroes on the graduate level, and a few undergraduates seeking specialized training not offered at Langston such as pharmacy or nursing education are admitted to colleges for whites as stipulated by the law, upon appropriate qualification.

Under this policy the institutions of Oklahoma were not authorized to admit Negroes to programs of study that were available at Langston; thus a situation of uncertainty was perpetuated during which legal opinions from the attorney general might need to be sought in borderline cases.

Fortunately, these uncertainties were removed on May 31, 1955, when the United States Supreme Court handed down a supplemental decision in the consolidated cases.[2] The Court unanimously reversed the lower courts, which had permitted racial segregation in public schools. It remanded the cases involved, with directions that the lower courts should be guided by equitable principles in "fashioning and effectuating the decrees" as defined in the Supreme Court's opinion. The high court stressed that the defendants should be prompt in complying with the decision requiring desegregation and that they would be required to show reason for delay in compliance—if such delay would be necessary in the public interest and consistent with good-faith compliance. The trial courts were directed to retain jurisdiction of the cases during the period of transition from segregated to desegregated conditions.

The State Regents for Higher Education acted promptly following the Supreme Court's decision of May 31. At a meeting on June 6, 1955, Regent John Rogers moved that

the governing boards and the respective presidents of the state-supported institutions within the state system of higher education are hereby authorized to accept qualified Negro students for admission effective at the opening of the fall term, 1955.

Rogers' motion was seconded by Regent Wharton Mathies, and it passed with one dissenting vote.

The events described in the preceding chapters seem, in retrospect, more like bad dreams than reality. Now it can be said accurately that *desegregation* at the Univer-

[2] 349 U.S. 294, 99 L.Ed. 1033 (1955).

sity of Oklahoma, once the Supreme Court finally made its momentous decision, was accomplished successfully and without perceptible resentment by the white members of the university community. However, *integration* of the races has been quite a different matter. Progress at the university, as in other institutions, has been slow and sometimes painful, hindered not only by the reluctance of whites to accept blacks completely in social and business activities but also by a growing inclination on the part of members of the black race to resist comingling, perhaps through fear of the loss of their cultural heritage. At the moment the latter would appear to be one of the principal barriers to the development of an integrated society and effective racial relations.

The several hundred blacks who attended the University of Oklahoma following the legal battles of the late forties made, on the whole, very good records as members of the student body. Perhaps they did as well, on the average, as white students, although there are no statistics that I know of that would throw any light on this question.

George W. McLaurin, unfortunately, was unsuccessful in his efforts to acquire a doctor's degree in education. He performed well in his classes, and he and Mrs. McLaurin, who also became a student, seemed to enjoy their attendance at the university. (Mrs. McLaurin had been the first of her race to apply for admission to the University of Oklahoma; she applied in 1923 and was refused.) But he was plagued by failing health as the time approached for his qualifying examinations, and it was finally necessary for him to withdraw.

Mrs. Fisher was liked and respected by all who knew her, and she became quite popular with the students and faculty in the School of Law. She received a bachelor of laws degree in 1951 and passed the state bar examination. She then entered into practice with the firm Bruce and Rowan in Oklahoma City, where she remained from 1952 through 1956. In 1956 she accepted an appointment to her alma mater, Langston University, as Director of Public Relations. About the same time she decided that she would like to work for an advanced degree in history at the University of Oklahoma, and she attended the institution during the summers for the next several years. She received a master of arts degree in history at the end of the summer session of 1968 and then became a teaching member of the faculty at Langston University in the Department of Social Sciences. She now serves as chairman of that department, in addition to teaching courses in history and prelaw.

While I was completing this chapter, I talked to Ada Lois by telephone in an effort to check my memory concerning certain events of the troublesome years. Not fully realizing the passage of time, I remembered a very attractive young girl who had sat in my office so many years before. After visiting with her for several minutes and having my recollection of several details pleasantly corroborated, I asked her how things had been going with her and if there were any "little ones" in her life. After a moment's hesitation she replied, "No 'little ones' in the sense I think you mean, Doctor Cross, but I do have two grown children and two grandchildren—who are very much a part of my life." Her firstborn is a daughter, Charlene Fisher Factory, a teacher in the Oklahoma City public school system and the mother of Ada Lois's two grandchildren. The other is a son named Bruce, who is now following in his mother's footsteps at Langston University.

This is the end of my story. It would not be proper to say at this time that "All's well that ends well," because the final results of the agony and turmoil described in the preceding pages are still not in sight. They lie beyond the horizon, and a great deal of forward progress must be made before they become visible. But the fact that there has been improvement in a difficult situation provides hope for continued progress. The first step, at least, has been taken in the right direction.

APPENDICES

APPENDIX I

In the Supreme Court of the United States
Monday, January 12, 1948.
No. 369—October Term, 1947.

Ada Lois Sipuel, Petitioner)	
v.)	On writ of Certiorari to
Board of Regents of the)	the Supreme Court of
University of Oklahoma, et al.,)	the State of Oklahoma
Respondents)	

Per Curiam.

On January 14, 1946, the petitioner, a Negro, concededly qualified to receive the professional legal education offered by the State, applied for admission to the School of Law of the University of Oklahoma, the only institution for legal education supported and maintained by the taxpayers of the State of Oklahoma. Petitioner's application for admission was denied, solely because of her color.

Petitioner then made application for a writ of mandamus in the District Court of Cleveland County, Oklahoma. The writ of mandamus was refused, and the Supreme Court of the State of Oklahoma affirmed the judgment of the District Court. _____ Oklahoma _____, 180 P.2d 135. We brought the case here for review.

The petitioner is entitled to secure legal education afforded by a state institution. To this time, it has been denied her although during the same period many white applicants have

139

been afforded legal education by the State. The State must provide it for her in conformity with the equal protection clause of the Fourteenth Amendment and provide it as soon as it does for applicants of any other group. *Missouri ex rel. Gaines* v. *Canada,* 305 U.S. 337 (1938).

The judgment of the Supreme Court of Oklahoma is reversed and the cause is remanded to that court for proceedings not inconsistent with this opinion.

The mandate shall issue forthwith.

Reversed.

APPENDIX 2

Judge Justin Hinshaw's Order in *Sipuel* v. *Board of Regents et al.*

IT IS, THEREFORE, ORDERED, ADJUDGED AND DECREED BY THIS COURT that unless and until the separate school of law for Negroes which the Supreme Court of Oklahoma in effect directed the Oklahoma State Regents for Higher Education to establish

with advantages for education substantially equal to the advantages afforded to white students

is established and ready to function at the designated time applicants of any other group may hereafter apply for admission to the first year class of the School of Law of the University of Oklahoma, and if the plaintiff herein makes timely and proper application to enroll in said class, the defendants, Board of Regents of the University of Oklahoma, et al., be, and the same are hereby ordered and directed to either:

(1) enroll plaintiff, if she is otherwise qualified, in the first year class of the School of Law of the University of Oklahoma, in which school she will be entitled to remain on the same scholastic basis as other students thereof until such a separate law school for Negroes is established and ready to function, or

(2) not enroll any applicant of any group in said class until said separate school is established and ready to function.

IT IS FURTHER ORDERED, ADJUDGED AND DE-CREED that if such a separate law school is so established and ready to function, the defendants, Board of Regents of the University of Oklahoma, et al., be, and the same are hereby ordered and directed not to enroll plaintiff in the first year class of the School of Law of the University of Oklahoma.

The cost of this case is taxed to defendants.

This court retains jurisdiction of this cause to hear and determine any question which may arise concerning the application of and performance of the duties prescribed by this order.

APPENDIX 3

Justice Wiley B. Rutledge's Statement of Dissent in *Sipuel* v. *Board of Regents et al.*

I am unable to join in the Court's opinion or in its disposition of the petition. In my judgment neither the action taken by the Supreme Court of Oklahoma nor that of the District Court of Cleveland County, following upon the decision and issuance of our mandate in No. 369, *Sipuel* v. *Board of Regents*, decided January 12, 1948, is consistent with our opinion in that cause or therefore with our mandate which issued forthwith.[1]

It is possible under those orders for the state's officials to dispose of petitioner's demand for a legal education equal to that afforded to white students by establishing overnight a separate law school for Negroes or to continue affording the present advantages to white students while denying them to petitioner. The latter could be done either by excluding all applicants for admission to the first-year class of the state university law school after the date of the District Court's order, or, depending upon the meaning of that order, by excluding such applicants and asking all first year students enrolled prior to that order's date to withdraw from school.

Neither of those courses, in my opinion, would comply with

[1] The mandate reversed the Oklahoma Supreme Court's judgment and remanded the cause to it "for proceedings not inconsistent with this opinion."

our mandate. It plainly meant, to me at any rate, that Oklahoma should end the discrimination practice against petitioner at once, not at some later time, near or remote. It also meant that this should be done, if not by excluding all students, then by affording petitioner the advantages of a legal education equal to those afforded to white students. And in my comprehension the equality required was equality in fact, not in legal fiction.

Obviously no separate law school could be established elsewhere overnight capable of giving petitioner a legal education equal to that afforded by the state's long-established and well-known state university law school. Nor could the necessary time be taken to create such facilities, while continuing to deny the required legal education to petitioner while affording it to any other student, as it could do by excluding only students in the first year class from the state university law school.

Since the state court's orders allow the state authorities at their election to pursue alternative courses, some of which do not comply with our mandate, I think those orders inconsistent with it. Accordingly I dissent from the Court's opinion and decision in this case.

INDEX

Administration Building (University of Oklahoma): 66, 67, 70, 93

Admissions Office (University of Oklahoma): 113; *see also* Ada Lois Sipuel Fisher, Oklahoma, University of

Agricultural and Normal University for Negroes: 11; *see also* Langston University

Amendments, United States Constitution: *see* Thirteenth Amendment, Fourteenth Amendment, Fifteenth Amendment

Anderson, Marian: 119

Arkansas, University of: 73

Assistant attorney general, state of Oklahoma: *see* Fred Hansen

Attorney general, state of Oklahoma: *see* Mac Q. Williamson

Bales, Jack: 68

Balyeat, Professor F. A.: 94

Bassett, George: 95

Beaird, Ted: 125; *see also* Oklahoma Memorial Union

Bender, John F.: 93

Benedum, Regent T. R.: 90

Bennett, Leo E.: 15

Bennett, President Henry J.: 78

Bizzell, President William Bennett: 9

Black Dispatch: 30, 56, 66; *see also* Roscoe Dunjee, Malcomb Smith Whitby

Board of Control for Langston University: 45; *see also* Regents for Agricultural and Mechanical Colleges

Board of Regents, University of Oklahoma: *see* Regents, University of Oklahoma, Board of

Boatman, State Representative Edgar: 111, 116

Bond, James: 65

Boyd, William S.: 56

Brandt, President Joseph A.: 5

Branham, David: 7, *see Wallace v. Town of Norman*

Brett, Tom: 70, 71

Broaddus, Judge Bower: 88

Brown, Justice Henry B.: 44; *see also Plessy v. Ferguson*

Brown v. Board of Education of Topeka, Kansas: 129

Bruce and Rowan (attorneys): 134

Bullock, Dr. W. A. J.: 35, 38

Bunn, Charles: 80, 83

Buttram, Regent Frank: 52; *see*

147

151

BLACKS IN WHITE COLLEGES

To
Betty and Bill Keown,
Long time good friends, with
warm personal greetings.
George T. Grove
Nov. 9, 1975